LEADING SCHOOLS II

G000153670

SENIOR MANAGEMENT TEAMS

ESSAYS IN LEADERSHIP
FOR CHANGING TIMES

Edited by
Brenda Despontin and Nigel Richardson

Published for the Girls' Schools Association and
the Headmasters'and Headmistresses' Conference
by John Catt Educational Ltd
2008

First Published 2008

Reprinted 2015

by John Catt Educational Ltd,
12-12a Deben Mill Business Centre, Woodbridge, Suffolk IP12 1BL
Tel: 01394 389850 Fax: 01394 386893
Email: enquiries@johncatt.co.uk
Website: www.johncatt.com

ISBN: 978 1 904724 59 9

Set and designed by
John Catt Educational Limited

Printed and bound in Great Britain by
The Charlesworth Press

CONTENTS

About the Contributors

Daphne West has had a career which includes working as head of modern languages at Sherborne School for Girls and Sevenoaks School; she has been a chief examiner for A level Russian and AS French, and has six Russian language textbooks to her name. Head of the Maynard School in Exeter since January 2000, she has continued something of a family tradition: her great-aunt, father and eldest sister were all head teachers. She is currently a member of the GSA National Council and has also served as an elected member of SHA/ASCL National Council. In her 'spare' time, she enjoys opportunities to walk on Dartmoor, and to make music: she directs a school choir, and currently sings with two award-winning west-country choirs.

Dr David Pacini is deputy headmaster of St Andrew's School, Bedford. He started his teaching career in the Boys' Division of Bolton School, before moving on to become head of biology and head of science at Haberdashers' Monmouth School for Girls. He is an experienced ISI inspector and was a chief and principal examiner in A level biology for two examination boards. He has delivered many INSET lectures and workshops on assessment and examinations to schools and at Bristol University, where he was a part-time associate tutor to students involved in initial teacher training at the School of Education. He is passionate for his pupils to learn and succeed and for staff to develop effectively – any colleagues interested in shadowing him can contact David at: dpacini@standrewsschoolbedford.com

Richard Backhouse is Principal at Monkton Combe School. He read economics at Selwyn College, Cambridge, before becoming a teacher quite by accident. He taught economics at Oundle, and then Bradfield College, to which he moved as head of department in 1996, and where he was director of pastoral and extracurricular activities, and subsequently housemaster of Hillside, before taking up his present role in 2005. He lists rowing, skiing, reading, Southampton Football Club and gadgets as his interests, but still finds (some) time for his wife and two children, who keep his feet firmly on the ground.

Dr Paul Chapman is an old boy of Latymer Upper School in Hammersmith and spent eight years at Gonville and Caius College, Cambridge, completing his PhD (on Jacobite propaganda) in 1984. He started teaching at Queen Elizabeth Grammar School, Wakefield, before becoming head of history and politics at Colfe's School in south-east London. He spent seven years at Royal Hospital School, Suffolk, where he was head of sixth form, before taking up the post of director of studies at Yarm School in 2003. His interests include walking, expeditions to remote places, good food and wine, film, theatre, jazz and Frisbee.

Charlotte Avery is Headmistress of St Mary's School, Cambridge. She was educated at St Paul's Girls' School and St Anne's College, Oxford, where she read English. After teaching English and drama at Newstead Wood School for Girls, Orpington, she moved to an equivalent post at South Hampstead High School, GDST, where she became second in department before transferring to Norwich High School, GDST, as head of English and drama and subsequently head of sixth form.

As deputy head (pastoral) at Highgate School, she oversaw its successful transition towards full co-education. She has undertaken inspection training and an MA in education management at King's College, London, and gained the NPQH qualification. She is also a member of the MOD's Research Ethics Committee.

Carol Richards has worked in independent schools for over 20 years, 16 of them in boarding roles. She has also been a head of department in business studies at St John's School Leatherhead and economics at Guildford High School. She is currently head of pastoral care, boarding and sixth form at Moira House Girls School, Eastbourne where she is the school's educational visits coordinator and she teaches economics and business studies. Carol is an assistant examiner for OCR (business studies). In her 'spare' time she is doing an MSc in educational leadership. During holidays, when she has time, she is a keen amateur genealogist.

Gerald Ellison is bursar and clerk to governors of The Perse School, Cambridge, having previously been director of finance and estates and assistant warden in the maintained sector. Educated at St Edward's School, Oxford, King's College School, Wimbledon, and Keble College, Oxford, (where he read English language and literature), he has been both a director and a company secretary in the commercial world. He is an independent school governor and a trustee of various charities, was certified as a recognised bursarial adviser for ISI inspections (until the role was abolished by ISI) and is on the panel of mentors for new bursars.

Thomas Packer is in his second Headship: as Headmaster of Teesside High School in Eaglescliffe near Yarm. He was educated at Kimbolton School and University College, Durham, where he read physics and mathematics. He completed a research degree: a mathematical treatment of musical acoustics using a green function technique. Prior to Headship he was deputy head of an HMC school, including a spell as acting head. His other teaching posts include Hereford Cathedral School where he was a housemaster and officer commanding CCF and head of science at Downe House. In 2001 he was elected a Fellow of the Institute of Physics. He serves on the further mathematics development group for the Mathematics in Education and Industry Project. He is a keen amateur musician and orchestral conductor and is a Lieutenant-Commander in the Royal Naval Reserve.

Christopher Jeffery has been the Head of The Grange School in Hartford, Cheshire (a relatively young HMC coeducational day school), since January 2005. Previous roles include deputy head and head of middle school at The Perse School, and housemaster at Bristol Grammar School, the school at which he was a pupil. A history graduate of York University, he spent two years as a musician and songwriter before committing himself to teaching, a choice that he only occasionally regrets. A Fellow of the Royal Society of Arts, he is married and has three children at The Grange. He retains a troubling and irrational attachment to Bristol Rovers.

Dr Helen Wright has been Headmistress at St Mary's School, Calne, since 2003. She is an Oxford graduate in modern languages and began her teaching career at Reed's School in Cobham (then all-boys), before working as a head of department and house tutor in co-educational schools: Bishop's Stortford College and St Edward's, Oxford. She made the move into girls' education at the age of 30, as deputy head (then acting head and Head) at Heathfield School, Ascot GSA. She is a firm believer in combining work and family; she has had young children and has completed her doctorate on moral leadership in schools during her tenure as Head at St Mary's.

Dr Brenda Despontin became Principal of the British School in Brussels in September 2008, having previously been Headmistress of Haberdashers' Monmouth School for Girls since 1997. She has a first degree in psychology, a masters' in Thomas Hardy, a doctorate in children's literature and an MBA on educational leadership. After teaching at The British School in Brussels and working as a residential supervisor in a home for disturbed teenage girls, she went on to teach at comprehensive and independent schools before setting up the girls' division at the King's School, Macclesfield. She was President of GSA in 2006.

Dr Nigel Richardson was Head of The Perse School, Cambridge 1994-2008, having been second master at Uppingham, Head of the Dragon School, Oxford and deputy head of the King's School, Macclesfield. He is a governor of several HMC schools, and was editor of the HMC magazine *Conference & Common Room* from 1999-2002. He has written history books for children and training literature for the Industrial Society, and contributes regularly to the educational press. He was chairman of HMC in 2007, and amongst other writing projects is currently working on a biography of the great Victorian headmaster Edward Thring.

Dr Stephen Coyne has been Head of Foundation at the King's School in Macclesfield since 2000, having previously been academic deputy at Whitgift School in Croydon. He is a chemist by training and was head of science at Arnold School, Blackpool, in the early 1990s. He previously also taught at The Manchester Grammar School, Merchant Taylors' School (Crosby) and Rainford High School.

He attended St Edward's College in Liverpool as a boy and is a published photographer and travel enthusiast, as well as a Head. He lives with his wife, Judith, and their two cats in Prestbury, Cheshire.

Introduction

Preparing the School Leaders of Tomorrow

Nigel Richardson

This is the second volume in the *Leading Schools* series. The first dealt with issues central to the work of serving Heads; this one is more focused (although not exclusively so) on those who are not yet in that role but who hope to be one day, and who may already be members of senior management teams (SMTs). Volume three will be concerned with academic and departmental leadership.

The chapters fall into two types. Early chapters chart the recent development of the roles of the various 'specialist' deputies (staff, academic, pastoral *etc*), which has been accompanied by the evolution of senior management teams. In the second half of the book we deal with a number of specific demands which could fall in various ways on either deputies or their Heads, and which follow on from the earlier volume on Headship. These too reflect the way in which school leadership has become a team effort (a theme explored in more detail by Daphne West in chapter 1). Behind this change lies the fact that deputies nowadays tend to fall into one of two broad categories.

The typical deputy in many independent schools (especially in the boarding sector) was once someone who had been at the school for many years, and who had come to the end of a fixed-term boarding house tenure or finished being a head of department (HoD). In an age with fewer administrative demands from beyond the school (censuses, policy statements *etc*), the role often centred around skills which combined Establishment and management figure, supporter of the Head, guardian of the ethos (within reason!), link with the former pupils, and common room senior figure-cum-confidante. This was, and still is, especially important just after the arrival of a new and inexperienced Head, when the existence of a wise and generous-spirited bridging figure between management and common room can make or break a new regime.

Of those in this category, some will have decided that they never wished to go on to Headship, or had left it too late. Others gradually decided that Headship was not, after all, something to which they aspired. Hugely valuable work is still done in many of our schools by this group. Either way, there may be issues about keeping yourself fresh and up to date through good and effective INSET. For both there are opportunities beyond the school itself: looking outwards and gathering information from the wider educational world through newspapers, websites and publications such as the ISC bulletins.

By contrast, over the past two decades, there has been a much greater tendency for schools to appoint deputies who harbour long-term ambitions. The deputy-cum-aspiring Head cannot be the common room confidante in the same way as the long-stayer, but this type of person too has to juggle many different aspects of the role. These include supporting your present school whilst looking to the future; getting rooted in your current community whilst knowing that you will probably be in the school for only a comparatively short span of years; spreading your wings and stretching your talents without getting under the Head's feet.

There is also the interesting phenomenon in what is often seen as a five-year career stage of the 'defining year three'. In the first two years, your new school (and its Head) capitalise on all the strengths which your addition to the team has given them – but it is often in the third year that the Head starts to sense whether this deputy is more than one-dimensional in skills-set and really does have the capacity to go all the way to Headship. In this year too, the deputy sometimes begins to find that he or she doesn't wish to, or doubts his ability to do so, after all.

For those aspiring to Headship later, by common consent, one of the hardest career hurdles in independent schools is the jump from housemaster or head of department to deputy head or director of studies – unless of course one is fortunate enough to be in the right place at the right time, and thus to be appointed from within. Where posts are externally advertised, the fields tend to be very big (much larger than for many Headships), and the competition is fierce. This is unsurprising, given that most GSA and HMC heads (especially in day schools), have now held a post of this type on their way to Headship: people rightly see being a deputy as the route to being a Head.

Personal experience can sometimes be illuminating: let me take you back 30 years to the days when second masters were invariably senior common room figures appointed from within, when director of studies posts were unknown, and when few new Heads even knew what a formal SMT was. One could wait months to apply for an SMT-type post. My first application to become a deputy (1979) went unanswered for several weeks. I emerged from a history lesson and took my courage in both hands, phoning the Head's secretary. "Oh, we appointed ages ago," she said, "180 applicants: we only interviewed mathematicians and physicists."

Shortage subjects, and the head start (no pun intended) which applicants offering these subjects enjoy, haven't changed that much; schools, especially smaller and un-endowed ones, are still tempted to get half of a teaching timetable out of such people if they can. I tried one or two more applications as vacancies occasionally arose, but was eventually fortunate (1983): a new Head in the school in which I was already working decided to break with tradition in his second master, by going for a 35 year-old. I was offered the post without advertisement, application or interview.

By 1992, a sea-change had taken place. The *TES* regularly carried a double page or more of such jobs. Senior management teams were now widely recognised as the order of the day, and the role of the deputy was recognised as part of a career progression involving much more than a *mind the shop when the Head's away* role.

In that year, after a brief spell in prep school Headship, I put myself into the senior school deputies' market once again. A dozen people made the long-list, and the school concerned organised a huge programme of interviews and visits to sort us out. There was a sizeable governor presence and, for four of us, the grilling was even more intense in round two a week later. I have met several of the others as Heads since.

So, there is now a proper career structure for school leadership. There is more career development – thanks to conferences for deputies, the growth of professional development courses run by IPD and others, and to the experience that many aspiring Heads have gained as inspectors during the first two cycles of ISI inspections. There are more opportunities to exchange experience via work-shadowing, cluster groups and GSA/HMC divisions, too. It may be that these developments – better training, greater opportunity to visit other schools, the rise of the 'five-year deputy' – explain why several leading schools recently have appointed Heads from within: something that would have been very unusual in earlier times.

Even so, the role of the deputy remains a fascinatingly complex one, insufficiently researched and written about. It combines (at different times) the role of purveyor of the party line (even when you have doubts about it) with that of filterer of ideas and complaints, whilst simultaneously being safety valve for frustrations about the Head and a shoulder to cry on when the Head is being difficult. Most Heads value having both a confidante and a sounding board, a sound day-to-day administrator, but someone who can also help with some blue-sky thinking. A few (unwise) Heads don't want much more than a cipher: others value the chance to use someone younger to fly kites and put a head over the parapet. Similar metaphors abound.

As deputy, you can sometimes feel deeply frustrated and powerless, convinced that the role of second-in-charge is, in the words of U S Vice-President (under Franklin D Roosevelt) John Nance Gardner, 'not worth a pitcher of warm spit'. For Nance it may have been true; he retired, leaving it to his successor, Harry S Truman, to take over when Roosevelt suddenly died. The man to whom he said those words, Lyndon B Johnson, experienced the same sudden elevation when John F Kennedy was assassinated. You can be just a heartbeat away...

You may be suddenly called on to preside over an interregnum between Heads, or to pick up the pieces when a Head suddenly departs without warning. Chapter 9 reflects on some aspects of this, and different people have different experiences in such situations. My own (1989: my then Head on sabbatical) was that staff were spectacularly supportive, but that

I had sometimes consciously to do things in the same way as the 'normal' Head would have done them, resisting the temptation to impose my own style on events too much.

By contrast, a very long-serving second master, pressed into acting Headship right at the end of his career during an interregnum between Heads, observed that the thing that surprised him most was how those who had been his colleagues up to then in an apparently united common room, used his brief time at the top to criticise each other fiercely to him in private.

Planned interim Headship seems to me to be an increasingly interesting issue. Legendary Heads who retire after a long time in office have often generated enough loyalty and goodwill for difficult issues to be shelved without rancour during their final years. The tensions sometimes surface once the legend has gone, if the unsuspecting newcomer is unable to satisfy everyone's individual agendas, all at once. On a research visit to the USA a few years ago, I was very surprised at how many schools appointed an interim Head (two to three years, usually just before retirement) to take the sting out of such a situation: the interim Head tackles the difficult personnel issues or does the controversial surgery, and then leaves the way cleared for the new permanent Head to hit the ground running. But I digress...

Could we do still more to prepare people for Headship? It is often observed that no-one, however able, can appreciate the full range of demands on a modern Head unless he or she has actually experienced it. There might be further ways of helping with this process. MBAs, MEds, the NPQH and courses run by the National College for School Leadership are increasingly seen as a good preparation for moving into Headship. Comparing regular notes with, or even shadowing, rising figures in major industries is another.

At a time when independent schools are being constantly encouraged to contribute time and expertise to emerging academies, could there be benefits both ways in seconding a deputy part-time to such a project? Of course there are implications of both time and cost, but the independent sector badly needs to face up to the parlous lack of secondment opportunities for its high-flyers compared with the maintained sector.

Should we be more proactive in encouraging other schools to appoint our deputies as their governors, rather than always turning to experienced Heads? Insight and experience of how governing bodies work, of their collective chemistry, and of how to channel governor expertise and enthusiasm is one of the most difficult areas of training, and too many new Heads have to learn it the hard way.

Again, there could also be two-way benefit. Yes, there are potential recruitment spin-offs for senior schools in having a serving Head on a prep school board, but we should not be afraid to admit that the right deputy might sometimes actually contribute more (maybe in valuably different ways to our own role as governors), and be able to attend its meetings more regularly.

Finally, Heads owe it to their deputies to spend a little money on proper external appraisals for them every two years or so (a theme covered by Keith Dawson in our previous volume). Headship appraisal is now well-established, and most of us who have been in Headship for a time know the benefits of being assessed by an objective, experienced outsider – and of being able to assess oneself and one's future career aspirations frankly and privately.

With so many deputies now carrying out appraisals of teaching staff themselves, being on the receiving end of an encounter with an experienced but unfamiliar appraiser can only be beneficial. Or – thinking more radically – is there scope for a pilot scheme within the independent sector consisting of external appraisal carried out not as a single major event, but as an ongoing process staged over a period of several years? It would have much in common with the arrangements for the NPQH qualification.

There are other reasons for external appraisal, too. If the Head and deputies are working really well together, the Head risks losing the cutting edge of detachment about those closest to him or her, which is an essential ingredient of any good appraisal exercise. After all, he or she chose them in the first place, and if the subsequent relationship has been a successful one, the Head's critical judgement may have been softened by a certain possessive pride in how things have turned out. It's often said that very longstanding Heads tend to gather around them governors who are too similar to themselves in both temperament and abilities; there are even greater risks of this within one's SMT. Ultimately if we really value those who work most closely with us, and if we hold to the view that the sector has a collective responsibility to give the best possible training to the school leaders of tomorrow, we should be able to find ways of facing up to the costs.

In the end, however, I have to admit that the ideas in the previous three paragraphs are a particular bee in my bonnet. External appraisal is not *the* major aspect of career development for the talented deputy: that role falls to his or her own Head – through the provision of a daily mixture of praise, guidance, constructive criticism, occasional brickbat and (above all) of experience of the maximum number of aspects of our multi-faceted job as can be arranged. Some Heads are much better (and more generous-spirited) at this aspect of their job than others. So, to return to some words which featured in our first volume (from a recent report for the DfES by PricewaterhouseCoopers LLP):

'The success of school leaders should be measured, not in terms of their impact on student achievement seen during their tenure, but rather on how many leaders they have developed and left behind who can go even further than they did.'

Chapter 1

The Senior Management Team

Daphne West

What's in a name? Probably not enough when it comes to the term 'senior management team', which nowadays usually indicates a group of people sharing the collective responsibility for everything from the management of day-to-day domestic details to the visionary leadership of a school. Whether a school has a 'senior leadership team' or a 'senior management team', you can be sure that the team will be involved in both leadership and management.

Certainly, the management structure of most independent schools today is far removed from the model which some of us may still remember from our earliest days in teaching – where the Head made unilateral decisions on matters academic, pastoral and domestic, usually with a single deputy as a conduit between the Head's study and the staff room. In its extreme form, this model tended to mean that development was slow and processes cumbersome, with little sense of connection between the staff delivering the pupils' education and the person at the top dictating what was to be delivered.

Of course, there are many examples in the history of education of wise and visionary Heads who, against the social and economic back-drop of their time, were able to direct their schools in a truly independent fashion and who made dramatic and positive changes in the lives of their grateful pupils and colleagues. A nineteenth- or twentieth-century Head was quite likely to lead a school for 20 years or more, and to have a vast knowledge of its pupils, staff, parents, rules and regulations – most of which was stored in a very considerable memory.

In the twenty-first century, we lead our schools against the back-drop of a society where communication, consultation and a collaborative approach are the order of the day, where people (including Heads) are likely to change their employment more frequently, where information is available in torrents to all, where external controls and checks abound in every area of our work and where we need to have our fingers on a whole range of pulses: academic and pastoral, financial, legal, marketing – and all this under the media's ruthless spotlight.

As a twenty-first century Head (I came into post in January 2000), daughter of a twentieth-century Headmaster and great-niece of a nineteenth-century Headmistress, I am deeply thankful that the concept of the senior management team was already well embedded in the British educational system before I started. Without the 'executive' group of senior colleagues who assist me in all aspects of leading and managing the school, I have no doubt at all that my position would be lonelier, my performance far less effective and my enjoyment of my role vastly diminished.

Working with the right team, whose members share the aim of providing the best possible educational experience for their current and future pupils, brings positive benefits to the whole school community. The SMT's work is a vital part of ensuring that conditions are in place for continuous improvement, that the predictable and the unpredictable are managed as smoothly as possible, and that exciting ideas are tempered, but not hampered, by realism.

What constitutes the 'right team'? Management guru Tom Peters gives a most useful rule of thumb: 'Leadership mantra number one: it all depends'. There can be no question of 'one size fits all' as far as the composition of an SMT is concerned, just as there is no one model of school which would suit every child in the land. Indeed, Heads will very probably find that, over the years, they refine the composition of the team, and the roles within it, in order to accommodate changing circumstances.

Truly, it *does* all depend – and on a variety of factors: the size, profile and overall ethos of the school, the particular challenges faced by the school at a given time and the nature of the expertise and experience of the staff. There is one common factor, however – and for this I return to

Tom Peters for another rule of thumb: 'Innovation is not optional'. The members of a school's SMT really do need to buy into this one. It may be old hat to say that schools have to be constantly aware of the impact of external developments as well as internal pressures, but it is nonetheless true. The capacity to enjoy engagement in independent, creative, flexible thinking is just as essential in an SMT as the sort of management skill which ensures that the school play doesn't clash with the regional hockey finals.

The Head's job is to lead the SMT, and the Head must therefore have a clear idea of what the team needs to make happen and which key players should be part of the team. For a Head new in post, this, ideally, is not something to be rushed: whilst the running of any organisation can always be improved, it is not wise to throw out the baby, bath water and most of the plumbing too rapidly – there will always be reasons for the constitution of a particular SMT and all sorts of wisdom and talents to be discovered. On the other hand, if the constitution of the SMT is clearly ineffective, it will be to the detriment of the organisation to struggle on without making significant changes.

So, what does the team need to make happen, monitor and review in the context of the school's size, profile, ethos, challenges and available resources? In a word – everything: the curriculum and all related matters, academic, pastoral and extra-curricular; the quality of the environment (everything from recruitment of staff to matters of health and safety); expectations of pupils, parents and colleagues. This presupposes a degree of relevant expertise and experience amongst the team, whose members need to gel if they are to achieve the best possible outcomes within the limitations of their time and the school's resources.

If the team gels, then feelings of purpose, motivation and satisfaction will characterise its work, which in turn will have a positive effect on the running of the school and the well-being of colleagues and pupils. The process of 'gelling' does not mean that the team will necessarily be of one accord on all issues – ideas need to be proffered, discussed, challenged and refined at SMT meetings, so a mixture of personalities and characteristics is definitely a plus: enthusiasm, caution, objectivity and imagination all have a role to play. On the other hand, the reluctance to offer individual opinions, the inability to limit one's own contributions to discussions, and the tendency to 'jockey for power' are decidedly negative factors in the SMT's capacity to manage and lead the school.

A pretty tall order, then: to put together a group of people who enjoy working with one another, who have the right areas of expertise and experience, who understand the need to be involved in discussion of areas of the school's activity in which they may not be immediately involved, who value the opportunity to take responsibility for particular areas of the school's work ... and who are prepared to stand up and be counted if some area of the SMT's work proves less than popular with other colleagues.

The single most important factor in the structure of the SMT is the kind of *balance* which ensures that the Head can maintain a clear overall view of the needs of the school, of how to address current problems and challenges, and of how future plans and projects will impact on the school community. It can be extremely helpful, therefore, to have a balance of academic and non-teaching colleagues in the team.

Take care, though, that the SMT does not become too large, and that its meeting time is a clearly scheduled and protected slot in the timetable; this is particularly important for academic colleagues (no good if the start of the meeting overlaps with the last ten minutes of the head of sixth form's teaching commitment or with the beginning of that important end-of-day slot when the head of juniors will be involved in meeting and greeting parents at the school gate).

The age range of a school will usually influence the academic constituency of the SMT, so that, for example, the various Key Stages can be represented (and for many people this may start at KS2 or earlier, through to KS5). The SMT roles taken on by the academic members of the SMT may well be largely shaped by the tasks identified in their job descriptions as deputy/assistant heads or as head of a particular Key Stage or faculty. The balance in numerical terms between academic and non-teaching colleagues may not be exact, but it is important that each area of the non-teaching organisation of the school is represented. One of the many lessons I have learnt during my headship is just how great is the importance of the work of non-teaching colleagues to the well-being of the pupils and the teaching staff.

In the context of my own school, I have found it enormously beneficial to ensure that the bursar, marketing and admissions manager and senior academic administrator are part of the SMT (while the first two of these posts will be familiar in most schools, the last may not: the responsibilities of our senior academic administrator include the management of the school's data base, diary, cover, examinations, and co-ordination of the departmental budgets of academic departments).

Whatever the nomenclature, the work of administrative, financial, and estate colleagues is represented on the SMT. For their part, the non-teaching members of my SMT tell me that their enjoyment of their job is enhanced by their greater understanding of the complexities of running the school, and by their increased awareness of the benefit the pupils derive from what is done in the school's administrative, bursarial and estate offices.

Conversely, the academic members of the SMT develop a clearer picture, for example, of the financial and legal aspects which sometimes constrain what we would like to do, as well as of the logistics involved in the support non-teaching teams contribute to the running of routine school events.

Of course, colleagues do not necessarily come as ready-made perfect SMT members, able and willing to formulate ideas and plans and to work cooperatively to turn these into practical working procedures. As leader of the SMT, the Head needs to be alert to imbalances in the way the team functions, as well as to ways of strengthening weaknesses.

The team is likely to function best if each member of the SMT, including the Head, is genuinely prepared to listen and to learn from one another; 'analysis paralysis' (and consequent lack of progress) is likely to occur if colleagues are in the habit of shredding every idea put forward – and this can be the case with the experienced expert ('we've tried that in the past and it didn't work') or the ambitious newcomer ('if we don't do this we won't be appealing to the modern parent and the modern pupil').

It is important to remember that potential weaknesses in team members can be balanced by their more positive qualities: so, for example, the colleague who is inclined to overlook practical details may also be the person who proffers the most exciting and imaginative ideas; the colleague who is indecisive under pressure may have a sensitive awareness of moods and situations in the school community; the soberly prudent team member with the least inspiring mode of delivery may have the most astute sense of judgement and discretion.

The SMT, then, should have an established structure, with clearly allotted roles and responsibilities. If it is to function well, the school community needs to know about the constitution of the team and to be clear that SMT members have clout. Much of the allocation of roles and responsibilities may flow naturally from each individual's job description (it would be very surprising if the bursar were not in charge of matters financial, and if the pastoral deputy did not lead on pastoral care), and there will be key areas which will concern at least one member of the SMT: quality of learning and teaching, staff welfare, assessment and reporting, appraisal and professional development of teaching and non-teaching staff, and so on.

Other important elements may have less obvious homes: who leads, for example, on a school's relationship with the community? Who co-ordinates the detail of the school's involvement in public benefit? Who liaises with the parents' association, with former pupils or with the school council? What about strategic planning, and planning for development and improvement?

Although it is not practical to have a vast SMT, this does not prevent a Head from involving other members of staff in SMT discussions when possible and appropriate. This can have lots of bonus points, including, for example: a) it can offer a golden opportunity to increase the sense of involvement of other 'stakeholders'; b) it can be a time-saving strategy in the checking of practical implications; c) it is a very good way of training up people for future SMT involvement; and d) last (but not least!) it can be a way of involving the staff room's resident 'coffee-cup manager' in real responsibility, even if for a short-term project (you know – the one who can't believe that "'*they*' (the SMT) haven't done anything about such-and-such an issue yet". Every staff room has at least one such...

Some of the SMT's business will arise naturally from the routine processes and events of the school year: the admissions process, open days/evenings, parents' meetings, public examinations, concerts, plays and sports days, to name but a few. All need to run as smoothly and happily as possible, and year on year the SMT should be seeking feedback and taking on board how such routine events could be refined and adjusted for the better. If each member of the SMT has clear roles and responsibilities, this helps enormously in suggestions and decisions about what other matters should be included in SMT meetings, and in what order of priority.

In my school we have finally evolved a system of building our agenda through the simple means of the team adding items (with an indication of importance or urgency) to the SMT meetings' folder on our intranet. We find this to be speedy and effective, and since each member of the SMT represents a certain section of the school community, no-one can object that there has not been an opportunity to influence what is taken forward.

A good deal of our work is governed by the unpredictable, and the SMT must also be ready to respond to, and learn from, unpredictable situations. These might be anything from the practical problems caused by a burst water main, to dealing with the trauma of a pupil's death, to the more routine complaints from parents, pupils, colleagues or the wider community. All such matters can be variously difficult, unpleasant or tedious to deal with, but usually there is something useful to be noted for future practice.

There will be moments when there is no consensus between SMT members, but when, for the good of the school, a specific decision must be taken. There can be no ducking this: the buck stops with the Head – quite literally, as the most highly paid member of the team, the Head bears the greatest weight of responsibility for decisions.

The Head must also ensure that a watchful eye is kept on the continuity of the SMT's work. Has discussion led to decisions? How are these decisions being implemented? What has the impact of these decisions been? How effectively is the SMT reviewing its work?

The concept of 'protected management time' is one which my own SMT is still learning to adopt in practice; each one of us has half-a-day of what is intended to be sacrosanct time when we can get on with our input to matters which deserve quality thinking time. Whilst we may choose to use this time in our offices, we are effectively off-site; given that no more than two members of a seven-strong team have PMT (an unfortunate acronym) at any one time, this means that should a crisis arise, there is still an ample senior presence. We have all discovered that considerable self-discipline is needed not to feel frustrated when our PMT slot coincides with a school function and not to give in to pressures 'just to fit in an appointment with a parent/colleague' in that temptingly vacant slot.

Finally, a question to test the robustness of the SMT structure and how well it functions: is the SMT strong enough to manage the school during the absence of the Head? If the absence is planned and predictable (*eg* an annual conference or participation in the inspection of another school), then the answer should certainly be 'yes'. But what if the Head is absent through some unpredictable personal crisis (illness, accident, family difficulty)? With a genuinely engaged and involved SMT, the answer should still be 'yes'.

Chapter 2

The Deputy Head as a Breed

David Pacini

Everything you wanted to know about deputy headship, but were afraid to ask...

"I suppose at a school like yours, you are the person in charge of everything?" enquired one of the delegates over coffee. Until six years ago we were teaching colleagues in the same school, but having gone our separate ways we were now re-acquainting ourselves whilst attending a conference in Westminster. Having answered that it sometimes feels like it, I set out to check the precise nature of the deputy head role to which my ex-colleague had just been appointed – a narrow brief concerning oversight of academic matters, but in a larger school than my own.

This conversation immediately came to mind when I was asked to contribute to this volume on school leadership. I must confess that initial exposure to the title of my task 'The Deputy as a Breed' brought out the biologist in me, as my mind flooded with images of different 'breeds' of deputy head I have known and respected. Do you recognise any of the following?

First, the straight backed, always soberly suited individual, never seen without jacket or clipboard/pile of paper and gliding effortlessly through the staff room, as an agile predator in search of prey. This breed of deputy always appears calm, issuing crisp expert advice and instruction in equal measure of politeness. Secondly, the affable, always chatty character; the male of this breed is never seen wearing a tie and both genders will be wearing a jacket only on the coldest of mornings. Characteristics of this breed include a steady pair of hands and awareness of your nutritional needs, by offering you tea or coffee and a selection from a dazzling choice of chocolates (where do they get them from?) and always the reassuring human touch.

Finally, perhaps you may have seen the more exotic plumage of the 'water cooler' deputy, instantly recognisable by a colourful display of designer suit and accompanying gender specific bow tie or eye-catching neck jewellery. This breed of deputy publicly multi-tasks in a courteous and apparently effortless manner, whilst encouraging discussion on a wide range of topics.

I hope the above tongue-in-cheek natural history lesson illustrates that it is actually very hard to define deputies as *a* breed. One thing is certain though: the individuals described above and, indeed, all of the deputy heads in our schools, possess highly developed skills and attributes, many of which they share in common, and which are essential to the successful performance of their duties.

Instead of attempting to define the deputy as a breed, it might instead be more profitable to describe the various niches and habitats which this particular animal occupies (sorry, last use of biological terminology!): what exactly does the role of deputy head mean?

The answer of course entirely depends upon the type and size of the school the deputy works in. For the benefit of colleagues who are taking the first step towards preparation for such a post – and I assume you make up most of the readers of this volume – we can place deputy heads into one of the following broad categories, many or all of which will probably be familiar to you:

- Academic deputy (or perhaps called a director of studies) – having oversight of all matters relating to the taught curriculum, timetable and examination results.

- Pastoral deputy – responsible for the welfare of all pupils, and may be the designated child protection officer.

- Staffing deputy – tasked with ensuring the professional development and wellbeing of staff.

- And, finally, the sole deputy – in charge of many or all of the previous areas of whole school responsibility, and likely to be found in a school of smaller pupil numbers than schools where the previous three categories of deputy are present.

In any one school, the deputy or deputies plus Head will form a large part of what is entitled either the senior management or senior leadership team. Many schools now embrace the latter title, not just as a semantic preference, but perhaps to reflect a changing and redistributed set of roles and responsibilities – the Head remaining as overall pacesetter and main leader, and deputies no longer just possible 'Heads in waiting' but needing to show leadership on a variety of issues to the whole school.

We shall read in immediately following chapters about the detailed demands made upon deputy heads with specific responsibility for the curriculum, staffing and pastoral welfare of pupils, but to set the scene for these contributors, I would like to share with you some of my own experiences – which by now you will probably have guessed have occurred as a sole deputy head in what ISC calls a 'small to medium sized' school.

Before I do that, here is my first piece of advice. It may seem obvious, but ignorance of it still trips up a surprising number of candidates for deputy head positions. Whatever else each deputy is responsible for, the key aspect of his or her role is to *deputise*. If you are uncomfortable with the thought of the many and public ways in which you will have to stand in for your Head, it may be that deputy headship is not for you.

In addition, each deputy is a vital bridge between the Head (and ultimately the governors) and the staffing body. Whilst being responsible for the school's current day-to-day operations and acting as the Head's bagman or 'Mr Fixit', a successful deputy must share his or her Head's vision for the future development of the school and show respect for the hopes and dreams, and occasional nightmares, of all other staff. We are both the Head's deputy and the staff's deputy.

What have been the key experiences for me as a deputy head? There have been many joys: an office entirely to myself, privileged access to the ear of the Head and the governors, increased secretarial support, a greatly reduced teaching load and the perhaps best of all, the chance to 'play at being a Head' with the knowledge that someone else is ultimately responsible for the actions of others and myself.

28

Yes, because of my changed role in relation to the common room as a whole, I do miss the occasional late Friday afternoon social drink with heads of department colleagues, but I can honestly say there have been no painful experiences, although some have come dangerously close and were often of my own making!

My role has certainly been as varied as I expected it to be. Indeed, one of the main reasons for applying for this job was deliberately to increase as much as possible the breadth of my experience of school life beyond what I now realise were the narrow confines of an academic subject department – even one that was very large and very successful. Despite welcoming the opportunity to be 'continuously professionally developed', I became convinced early in my first term that whenever my Head was away from school on inspection duty or attending a GSA conference, she had deliberately set up a series of extremely tricky and difficult problems for me to tackle.

In almost my first day of 'deputising' there was an urgent phone call relayed via reception from a parent whose daughter was not answering her mobile phone and was probably now embarked on a bus journey that would leave her stranded in the countryside, without a lift home. My phone rang when I was in the middle of replying to an important, and just received, email from the chairman of governors, and only two minutes away from the start of the senior school staff meeting. A good in-tray exercise!

Then there was the interesting Friday lunchtime when, having just been informed that there were insufficient staff to run today's after-school club, I was literally intercepted by a parent in reception who demanded to see me about an urgent issue, when already on my way to a scheduled meeting with another parent...

Several more days like this presented themselves in rapid succession. They led me to expect a flashing red light and buzzing alarm sound to start making their presence known, rather like in the 'cockpit' of a flight simulator, and for the wall of my office to slide away, revealing a grinning headmistress and her secretary, both of whom had been masterminding proceedings.

How could I have been prepared for these experiences? During my first few weeks at my new school I had rigidly followed the advice from one teaching friend before starting my senior leadership career, who exhorted me to "keep your jacket on and occasionally be rather unreasonable", but this had not helped me escape these situations. Instead, a rather different sugestion from a deputy head at my previous school of "you will need to develop the ability to speak to two different people about two different issues at the same time…" seemed to fit the bill. Unfortunately, I hadn't counted on having to become so proficient so soon.

However I survived and no-one else came to any harm. The qualities of sound judgement and sense of proportion under pressure and the ability to prioritise and delegate, which I must have shown to at least some degree in my interview to have gained this post, had not completely deserted me.

I had also learned which colleagues to trust and lean on when assistance was needed. These experiences also showed me what everyday life is like for a Head: scheduled tasks and appointments being regularly interrupted by unexpected and often urgent events. This is what it is really like to sit in the Captain's 'big chair' and be ultimately responsible for the running of the entire ship.

Of course, my preparation for a senior leadership role had begun, as it does with all deputy heads and Heads, with my first teaching post. It is in those first few busy and tiring terms that so many of the work and personality traits, which are essential for successful leadership and management, are developed and honed. Management of a large teaching department allowed further development – including how to delegate tasks realising, often the hard way, that it is simply too tiring and counterproductive to attempt to complete everything oneself.

Talking at length and at regular intervals to Heads and deputies at my first two schools allowed me to see how human they really were, and that they experienced many of the same pressures of work that I did. Most importantly I could see how they coped with these pressures, whilst maintaining a sense of proportion and humour and genuinely supporting each other as teams. If you are starting to think of deputy headship, I would urge you to seek out your senior colleagues for similar discussion.

Progression from middle management to senior management has often anecdotally been described as the hardest promotion to achieve. Mathematically, so it should be, given the large number of possible heads of subject departments or heads of year who are eligible to apply for a single senior academic or pastoral post respectively. There is not the degree of limitation on the field of candidates, which occurs when the post of head of a specific subject department is advertised, or indeed, when a Headship is to become vacant.

How then can a candidate help to make him or herself stand out in a large and competitive field, and at the same time learn something (s)he will find useful if successful in the application? Attendance at one or possibly two courses aimed at preparing teachers for a senior role will be time well spent. Excellent courses are run by the IPD organisation of HMC and GSA, but do not ignore the very high quality provision aimed primarily at the maintained sector. Attending such a course focused my mind on the requirements of deputy headship and helped me sharpen the skills and attributes I needed to produce a more effective application and interview performance.

Undertaking a part-time or distance learning postgraduate qualification in educational management or leadership will also broaden and deepen your understanding of whole-school issues beyond your current academic or pastoral specialism. Do not be afraid to continue learning; having enrolled on such a course I quickly realised how invalid was my arrogant view that my First Class Honours Degree and PhD meant I had no need of further study.

If you have further ambitions of Headship, do consider the revamped NPQH qualification: although it is now designed for candidates who should gain a Headship within 18 months of starting the programme, I suggest that even a quick glance through the NPQH application form will help you direct your energies into acquiring the full range of competencies and experiences that are deemed essential for success – in the maintained sector at least.

Finally, do apply to become, or continue to be, an inspector for ISI. I have yet to meet anyone who has not felt this experience to be one of the very best, or indeed *the* best, form of professional development for aspiring and serving deputies and Heads.

If you are sure that deputy headship is for you, but you are unsure of the precise role or the type or size of school you wish to operate in, try to visit a school, different from your existing one, to observe a deputy at work. At the beginning of this year I hosted a head of department from a school whose Head I had worked with on an inspection team. Following in the footsteps of the very successful GSA Head Shadowing Scheme initiated by Brenda Despontin, we arranged for this head of department (who is just starting to think of preparation for a more senior role) to observe me at work for a full day. We both found the day very profitable and I have since been 'shadowed' by several other heads of department from different schools. I certainly wish I could have been a shadow a few years ago.

Having undertaken some professional development and decided upon the type of school and type of deputy head role you wish to perform, study the job description and person specification carefully before deciding to apply for an advertised post – but not just in terms of the basic responsibilities and requirements. More importantly, do you recognise anything of yourself in the list of desired personality characteristics? Is the school looking for the same *breed* of deputy head that you think you will become? Can you see yourself working daily with the Head: sharing the most confidential information about pupils, staff and parents, debating strategy and policy and being able to find suitable moments to share a joke?

So, I have attempted to give you a whistle stop tour through deputy headship – what the role involves for me personally; how one might seek to prepare for the role; and how beneficial such preparation and eager advice from colleagues has been for me. A favourite interview question often takes the form of "What has been the most satisfying aspect of your current role?" For me, the highlight has been the high degree of autonomy given to me by my current Head – letting me know in advance that she will fully support decisions I might take in her absence and then sticking to this guarantee upon her return to school. Without doubt this has given me increased confidence in my leadership ability and consolidated my desire for a Headship of my own.

What final pieces of advice might I now pass on to aspiring and recently appointed deputies? In the detective novels of Reginald Hill, Peter Pascoe often thinks of himself as 'the ultimate chameleon' – selecting the appropriate blend of interpersonal skills to allow a full and successful dialogue with different types of people. Psychologists would say that this is displaying a high degree of 'emotional intelligence'. Perhaps using his or her 'emotional intelligence' would not be out of place for a deputy head having to communicate with the exciting and disparate personality types who are our common room colleagues. (I am not suggesting by the way, that all Heads should exhibit the type of personality or language used by Peter Pascoe's superior officer Andy Dalziel, although the occasional use of particularly blunt speech can be very effective!)

Always communicate to your Head everything you receive from staff, pupils and parents. Yes, you may well need to pick your moment, and certainly your choice of words, on any potentially critical matters, but you must find a way. I realise other deputy head colleagues may disagree, but I can think of no good reason not to do this. Even apparently trivial items can suddenly become connected to other pieces of information the Head has been made aware of by other people – the picture on the jigsaw will then start to appear…

Try to plan ahead and think of all the possible consequences of your decisions, but don't worry too much if you make mistakes: everyone does from time to time. The important thing is to limit any damaging fallout, not just to appear to cover your own back, but for the welfare of others affected by your action or inaction, and for your future credibility. If a pupil or member of staff sees that you care, and that you are trying to put things right, they are much more likely to trust you with a future problem – one that could be absolutely vital.

Don't forget the alternative three Rs: Realism, Resilience and Resourcefulness, although Ruthlessness may need to appear at some time. Most important of all, heed the advice given to me before taking up my current role: leave time for yourself and your family.

Whatever stage of your career you find yourself at now, I hope your time as a deputy head is as enjoyable as mine. Good luck!

Chapter 3

The Staffing Deputy

Richard Backhouse

According to haysmacintyre's management survey of the independent schools' sector, teaching costs for 2005-6 absorbed 52.5% of net fee income. This figure not only highlights the importance of teachers, but also confirms that they are a school's biggest and most important resource: they need to be trained, nurtured, guided and occasionally steered in new directions. The leadership and management of them is a crucially important task. Recruiting the right staff will have more impact on teaching and learning than any policy.

The staffing deputy is thus a key member of the SMT. The scope and title of the role vary: in many schools it is combined with that of senior deputy, while the term 'second master' is often used in boys' (or formerly boys') schools. The relationship with the Head will be crucially important: meetings will be frequent and very open, advice will be sought – in both directions – and delegation will include issues of great importance and sensitivity.

Very high levels of trust are essential, and large quantities of information will flow back and forth. The staffing deputy will often have to make decisions on the spot, so the Head must be willing to be asked for retrospective approval, sometimes even forgiveness – and only rarely for permission. The staffing deputy should expect public backing from the Head in everything too: they should disagree only in private.While the pages that follow deal with the detail, these essential principles underlie the relationships between the two of them – and their many and varied daily interactions.

The staff handbook, or staff manual, is the personal fiefdom (and *bête noir*) of the staffing deputy. While I waited for my final university holiday to elapse, I received in the post an A4 brown envelope from the school whose teaching staff I was about to join. It contained a vast array of sheets of miscellaneous policies.

I was instructed to read these, and to make sure I was familiar with them. I remember the various documents being interesting, in the same way that the menu of a mediaeval monastery would be interesting: they depicted a life of which I had so little idea and experience that the requirements were far too remote to be absorbable.

These days, of course, these policies are collected into a single work: that staff handbook. As a collected work, it ought properly to be more coherent, and more useful than the collection I received in the summer of 1990. This is just as well, because, since that date, the expectations which schools have of their staff, and the litigious nature of parents, have changed so dramatically that staff cannot afford the long and gentle run-in which I enjoyed, teaching, for example, only two examined sets in my first year!

The assorted policies that I inherited were the domain of the deputy head, who, in a school of more than 100 teaching staff, also looked after all routine activities, all staffing issues, all appraisal, and absolutely anything day-to-day which didn't fall within the purview of the director of studies.

Fortunately the increase in the demands of this latter role has coincided with such an increase in importance, specialisation and workload, that larger schools at least will have a greater degree of senior staffing available to complete the overall task – backed up, too, by much more clerical help than would once have been the case. In smaller schools, however, a deputy may still have a very broad remit.

The handbook is the most visible part of a staffing deputy's role, and often the most influential. It is the equivalent to the technical guide in an aircraft cockpit: when something is amiss, it should have the answer. Yet the handbook should never be seen as the determinant of the level of competence of the staff: it merely establishes the minimum acceptable level of completion of many aspects of school life.

While schools rely on relationships to accomplish the development of young people, and informal lines of communication may allow for excellent staffing of a school, the handbook describes the systems a school employs to achieve its ends in order to prescribe a *floor* to the conscientiousness and rigour which staff may bring to bear on their day-to-day school activities.

Two important sets of considerations need to be addressed before a handbook is started or reviewed. First, at whom is the handbook aimed? And secondly, how will it be used? The readership – diverse, in this case, with different purposes – is the essential determinant of whether or not the handbook will achieve its objectives.

Staff will read it *in toto* when they join, and – if you are lucky – they will return to it from time to time; they will consult parts of it when they think refreshing their understanding of a particular issue is advisable.

But you cannot expect new staff to take it in all at once: induction needs to be broken up into manageable chunks, and they need to be led through the handbook – ideally via a number of sessions before the first term begins, and then in follow-up meetings thereafter. Two key criteria are that the handbook should be clear, and easily navigable. A digital version with hyperlinks from one related section to another is a great advantage in this respect.

Different schools will group their policy statements and other expectations in different ways in the handbook. But school inspectors are also going to be interested readers of it. For them, there are particular topics that will need to be included in order to satisfy the relevant regulatory requirements. Briefly, these are policies to

- prevent bullying, (*cf* DfES Guidance 'Bullying: don't suffer in silence');

- safeguard and promote the welfare of children who are pupils at the school (*cf* DfES Guidance 'Safeguarding Children in Education' [DfES publication number 0027/2004]);

- safeguard and promote the health and safety of pupils on activities outside the school (*cf* DfES Guidance 'Health and Safety of Pupils on Educational Visits');

- promote good behaviour amongst pupils;

- set out the sanctions to be adopted in the event of pupil misbehaviour.

And further, policies on:

- health and safety on the school site, including fire;

- first aid;

- admissions and registration;

- the curriculum;

- equal opportunities;

- the school's complaints procedure.

Other key policies include:

- drugs and procedures for drugs testing;

- alcohol;

- learning difficulties/special educational needs;

- disability;

- data protection;

- code of practice for staff;

- pupil concerns/complaints.

In addition, the following might make a useful checklist of other policies, although the reader should take this to be like the Apocrypha – interesting but not authoritative! It too is far from exhaustive:

Staff absences
Job descriptions for senior staff
INSET and staff development
Duties
Disclosure whistle blowing
Communications
Policy for pupils missing from school
The tutor system

Private use of school resources
Policy for teaching pupils on their own
The role of prefects
Assessment
Coursework for public exams
Parents meetings
Visitors access to school premises
Sports policies and options
CCF
Meningitis emergency planning
Accident and injury
Emergency procedures
The medical centre
Minibus
Guidance on pupil welfare to host families
Policy for extras on fee bills
Insurance
Travel expenses
Use of force to control/restrain pupils
Records retention
Data protection

As well as inspectors and the school's staff, two further stakeholders are important. First, governors should receive the handbook when joining the board: it is the single document which will guide them most in the expectations that they may have of the day-to-day professionalism of the staff. It will also reassure them (when they most need it) of the rigour of the school in areas such as health and safety.

Lastly, the Head will need the handbook, especially when dealing with staff disciplinary issues – occasions when the effectiveness of policies may be very closely examined (but not the only ones when this tends to happen!). For this reason, it is strongly advisable to ask staff to sign and return a slip to say that they have read the handbook at periodical intervals – not just when they have recently joined the school, but also after major policy reviews and changes. It is imperative that management and staff both understand that the function of the handbook in this respect is to establish a baseline of acceptable professionalism; it should never be taken as the ceiling, only as the floor!

Three final points apply to the writing and editing of the handbook:

1. Clarity – both of expectations and of communication, even to the point of teaching granny to suck eggs on both points.

2. Comprehensiveness – even to the point of tediousness: it is much better to think of everything at this stage, than to regret it after an omission is exposed by events.

3. Accessibility – even to the point of being as all-embracing a source of knowledge as the Microsoft help icon.

It could be argued, of course, that it is hard to achieve the second and third of these criteria simultaneously...

In order to achieve the characteristics above, it is recommended that the handbook is arrived at by the following stages:

1. Initial writing.

2. Consultation.

3. Re-drafting: the importance of the handbook being a living document cannot be overstated: it is reasonable to compare it to Wikipedia. A school's intranet ought to be an enormous help in this respect.

Finally, a wise commentator on independent school staff once observed that most common rooms are made up of managerialists, a-managerialists, and anti-managerialists. The first will see the handbook as establishing all change: if it is in the handbook, everyone will do it. The second group will see the handbook as an unnecessary and burdensome document that prevents the inspirational teacher from doing his/her job to best effect. The third will see the handbook as a pernicious device, by which members of staff can be persecuted, or through which the golden age of private and independent education is put at risk. All three views are equally dangerous!

What are the key principles which lie behind the process of selecting staff?

The NCSL Safer Recruitment Course is strongly recommended. No-one should be appointed to the teaching or support staff without the involvement of at least one person who has undertaken this training. In the post-Bichard report world, to make an appointment without the active inclusion of someone so trained would (rightly) be seen as unnecessarily risky.

Whilst issues of teaching ability might seem to be the most important in the appointment process, the safety of young people is a duty higher than competence. It is imperative that the agreed process includes specific measures to ensure that this is the case, and that any variation (for example, to recruit for maternity cover, or for a very part-time teacher to cover a bulge in numbers in one A level subject) does not exclude those careful means by which a school may be as sure as possible that the appointee does not pose a risk to children or young people.

As a general rule – if you have any choice over timing – aim to recruit senior staff before Christmas (which enables you to have a second trawl if you don't find what you want first time), and for more junior posts from January. PGCE students don't usually start looking for jobs in earnest until at least the New Year, but many of the best ones will have gone well before Easter.

Advertisements, and the decision to make appointments, will normally be decided by the Head. Persuade the bursar at the outset that the new post is essential, too: there is no quicker way to lose the trust of a bursar than to appoint a member of staff for whom no provision is made in the budget. Plan the process and its timetable carefully, working backwards from the final post-interviews wash-up to share feedback, followed by an hour of the Head's time to make the requisite phone calls, to the external deadline for the advertisement and the internal deadline for the details booklet or job description.

There is a significant breadth of opinion on good practice in advertising, but the key decision about the advertisement itself is what to include. It is worth including a phrase indicating that child protection procedures at the school are robust, and that interview and selection includes background checks. Beyond this, everything is a matter of opinion, but people in the HR industry often comment that advertisements for teachers more often resemble public notices, with too much detail.

The sole function of the advertisement is to encourage the maximum number of potential applicants to ask for the details of the post, with a view to preparing an application. There are now plenty of different media for the advertisement, including the traditional *TES*, the *TES* online and other web-based media – all effective in different ways.

The key is to maximise the number of potential employees passing through each stage of the funnel: the advertisement only has to result in applicants asking for details, the details must maximise the number applying, and so forth. Clearly, some filtration can be beneficial – it is no good having applications from those fundamentally unqualified for the post!

Detail packs are the school's first opportunity to impress the would-be applicant. The more information they include, in particular answering the questions that an applicant might be asking, and the better prepared they appear, the more chance there is of the school succeeding at this crucial stage of advertising itself to the applicant.

It is sensible to include a description of the school, of the immediate environment of the post (such as details of the department in which the applicant will be working), the job description of the post advertised, equal opportunities policies, and the basis of payment of expenses. It is reassuring to the applicant if the details also include the likely programme of interviews for the post. This author has found it helpful to include in the details the likely date(s) of interview, since this can lead to early disclosure of dates when the interviewee is unavailable for interview.

Internally, there is always a need for openness and transparency. It is worth drawing the attention of existing staff to all posts which are being externally advertised: they may possibly know of a good candidate. It is good practice to advertise all middle and senior management posts internally too: existing staff will want to feel that internal applications are welcome, even though they will sometimes feel that an external appointment is a foregone conclusion.

Most schools will take considerable steps to ensure that the interview process shows the school at its best. All applicants are going to return to their own staff room, PGCE course or university with an account of your school, and you may well benefit from the opportunity to recruit someone else from those places, even if this particular applicant is not right for the post advertised. It is harder than it might seem to ensure that interviewees are asked different questions by different interviewers, and to ensure that no one ever asks the questions which might give rise to a discrimination allegation (for which, of course, there is no maximum payout!).

Consider whether or not you wish to ask candidates to teach a lesson (surely a *sine qua non* for any junior or middle management position these days), whether to use in-tray exercises *etc*. For a senior pastoral position (*eg* head of the sixth form), think about how far pupils might be involved – either via tours of the school or a candidates' lunch. It probably goes without saying that the staffing deputy will need to be well versed in all the questions about ISCtip induction procedures, QTS standards *etc*, that candidates may ask, and that a key part of the role is steering young teachers through these qualifications once they have been appointed.

There are two great dangers of recruitment: the first is the temptation to make an appointment out of a disappointing field. There is great truth in the old maxim 'Appoint in haste: Repent at leisure'. It is much better to re-advertise, if you are in any doubt as to whether there are any candidates you really want to appoint.

The second pitfall is to ignore your future member of staff, once the appointment has been agreed. If your new recruit simply fails to arrive at your school, your legal or other recourse is very limited. Appointment is the beginning of a process and, while the school might be able to sigh with relief at a job completed, it can be the beginning of an anxious period for the appointee. Best, therefore, if there is a planned sequence of communication with the appointee, managed by the person who will be their line manager when they arrive.

Induction is not only important, but is increasingly seen as an essential part of normal best practice, particularly in a boarding school. It may be one of those areas where traditionalists will opt for a minimalist approach. It is certainly the case that much should be delegated to the head of department or other line manager, but other induction should be conducted centrally for all members of staff. The process should include a session with:

- the Head – to explain the school's mission statement;

- key pastoral managers – either a deputy, head of year or houseparent: to elaborate lines of communication, and the key do's and don'ts;

- the academic deputy – to outline the vital academic requirements of the first few days;

- the chaplain, or equivalent senior non-management member of staff, to make clear where to go for a listening ear.

Whilst practical matters can usually be assigned to a head of department, we have found it useful to ensure that there is a central checklist of essential items (establishing a 'floor' again) which all HoDs should cover. Some departments (for example, chemistry) will need time when departmental protocols and health and safety issues can be explained, too. It is important that the beginning of term arrangements allow for the meetings that will be required for this.

Business theory indicates that communication which takes place along informal lines is often more effective than the formal communication structure of the organisation. How wise, then, the mentor who sent me, on my first day in the town where I was to teach my first classes, and long before the pupils had returned, the advice to introduce myself to the Head's PA, the school secretary and the bursar's secretary.

I had strict instructions to ingratiate myself, because "whatever you need to know, one of them will always know the answer, or where to find it". It was advice I felt, when I left six years later, to have been among the best I had received. Induction needs to impart advice like this: guidance that only mentors with plenty of experience, and some cynicism, will impart! The a-managerialists, again!

Many Heads will delegate, or consult extensively with the staffing deputy, on internal appointments of minor responsibility such as the running of a school magazine, or the resident tutorship in a boarding house. It is often invaluable for a staffing deputy to be able to have a quiet word in the ear of a colleague, establishing that they are interested in a role, even if the Head is the one who later closes the deal.

Deputies can conduct informal conversations of this sort beside the photocopier, with far less charge or stress than will be present in the Head's office, and the deputy can also employ the ancient tactic of saying, "Don't give me an answer now, think about it for a couple of days". I well remember being reeled in over a period of three weeks by a deputy who knew that my initial response would be negative, but suspected that giving me time to brew might elicit a more positive answer!

The staffing deputy will often also manage appraisal, although it may also commonly be run by a 'senior teacher' figure, who is not on the SMT and therefore has a more detached role in the eyes of the teaching staff. Most staff have experienced a high number of appraisal systems – few policies change more often in a school, which is a good sign that it is near impossible to find the perfect system. Observation of many systems suggests that one should aim for:

- Simplicity: if the staff cannot understand the process easily, they will get lost in it. It ought to be possible to explain it on one side of A4 without resorting to small print.
- Efficiency: if forms are to be used, reduce them in size so that the result is not verbose – no one enjoys an appraisal process so time-consuming that it reduces levels of performance.
- Bite: too many appraisals are concluded in language so encrypted that the appraiser does not receive the signals being given by the appraisee, nor the appraisee by the appraiser.
- An expectation of professionalism: since we are professionals, there must be a degree of self-appraisal involved. We can hardly be expected to teach young people to be independent learners if we are not teaching our own staff to be so.

For this reason, I strongly endorse a system in which staff appraise themselves first, on unequivocal scales, are then appraised on the same scales by their line manager(s), and have clear training needs identified, either to improve weaknesses, or to prepare them for the next role they might take on.

A detailed analysis of appraisal is a topic for another day (see also volume 1, *Heads*, in this series), but meanwhile suffice it to say that appraisal and INSET work need to be closely linked, that the purposes of appraisal must be clearly worked out by the SMT, and that it should include an element of empowerment for all staff to take some responsibility themselves for their role in their professional development.

For the staffing deputy, this next role may often be a headship of his/her own. The preparation this role affords is good, but it should also be enjoyable in its own right. Nevertheless, it is not unusual for those charged with the development of other staff to overlook their own development, and this is unwise, even if it is noble – not least because senior staff need to model to other staff the importance of continuing to learn themselves.

Ultimately, the staffing deputy's job is one much to be envied: theirs is usually the most senior post in a school in which friendly and collegiate relationships with fellow-teachers are not yet changed beyond recognition by seniority. This situation is not open to Heads – savour it while you can!

Chapter 4

The Academic Deputy/ Director of Studies

Paul Chapman

The role of the academic deputy or director of studies exists in some form in all schools, but there is considerable variation between each one. Sometimes the role is divided, or parts of it are devolved, but potentially it is enormous: no less than responsibility for the whole of academic life and progress in the school. In other words, it is an immensely exciting and challenging job.

Generalisations always contain with them some untruths, but an overall impression is that there has been a shift in emphasis from statistics, data and timetabling – important as all of these are – towards management of academic departments and oversight of pupil performance. This is logical because, to twist the words of an old proverb, simply measuring a pig doesn't fatten it. Some schools nowadays are making the distinction between teaching and learning, dividing the role between two academic specialists. Whether the goal is the improvement of examination performance or the provision of high quality education, the academic deputy has a key role to play. In industry it would perhaps be seen as the quality assurance role.

The relationship with heads of department is all-important in managing academic departments. It presents many challenges. In some schools the number of separate heads of department is potentially overwhelming. The practicalities of getting to know, and providing support for, perhaps 20 or more middle managers are immense. The alternative, of having a smaller number of senior heads of department or heads of faculty, has advantages in terms of the number of people to deal with, but it imposes another layer of management that potentially cuts off the academic deputy from the foot soldiers in the trenches.

There has to be a balance between two things. First, acting on the one hand as the supporter and champion of the head of department who, if your selection process is right, is an expert in his or her own field, and is dedicated to providing the very best for pupils in that area. Secondly, challenging and questioning that head of department to ensure that he/she is getting the best from the members of it. Much of this comes down to natural leadership style. Encouragement and praise go a very long way. It is a rare head of department who doesn't appreciate interest in what the department is doing, a supportive presence and an opportunity to talk over the issues.

Confronting underperformance, whether by the department as a whole or by its leader, is the biggest test of the academic deputy. Few of us enjoy initiating a situation which can be distressing to all involved. In the end, however, what we do as school leaders has to be guided by what is in the best interests of the pupils in our care who, after all, only get one chance at each stage in their education. They deserve no less than our very best endeavours.

There is a serious shortage of formal training available for tackling these situations, but experience suggests a few guidelines:

- Always deliver difficult messages face to face.

- Make sure of your brief. Be ready to support your points with clear evidence.

- Take advice from the Head and senior colleagues. Consider consulting a subject expert from another school; the academic deputies' network can be invaluable in this respect.

- Be clear in advance what outcome you wish to achieve. Is this in any sense a disciplinary meeting? In which case particular rules apply. Is it meant to be an informal nudge in the desired direction?

- Arrange the venue and time of the meeting so as not to be interrupted.

- Try to depersonalise issues. Comment on events, procedures and outcomes rather than people.

- In difficult situations asking the question 'What is in the best interests of the pupils?' can be a powerful tool.

- Allow the opportunity for evidence or views to be offered from the other side. A head of department has the right to be listened to, even if you don't ultimately agree.

- Ensure that there is a clear conclusion to the meeting. This may be to allow time for further reflection or for gathering more evidence. Alternatively, it may be that the meeting concludes with a clear decision or instruction from you, in which case it is essential that it is communicated unambiguously and unequivocally.

- Consider whether you should follow up the meeting with a written communication. This can be helpful in clarifying things which may have been perceived as inflammatory.

Managing regular meetings of the heads of department is one of the key tasks of the academic deputy. This too can appear extremely daunting in schools where HoDs are numerous and where some of them may be eager to seize any opportunity for axe grinding. On the one hand people should feel they have a chance to express a view, and you certainly want to find out what they really think. On the other hand you lose the goodwill of the many if you allow the few to waffle on.

As a result of years of being on the receiving end of frustrating meetings, here are some suggestions:

- Always circulate heads of department in advance to ask for items for the agenda. They may or may not supply things, but at least you can insist that they've had the opportunity. It's also a chance to ensure that the menu on offer is not solely you talking!

- Prioritise items for discussion and explicitly allocate set amounts of time for each item. Stick to this schedule and insist on moving on.

The majority will be very grateful to feel the meeting is making progress and to be able to predict when it will finish.

- Consider whether you really need to start with 'Matters Arising'. Yes, it *is* conventional, and it has the advantage of showing a follow-up to the previous meeting. On the other hand it is often a very depressing start, especially when it drags on for ages. Instead why not write those items you want followed up explicitly into the agenda?

- Shift mere routine administration to the back end of the meeting, or deal with it by way of memo instead.

- Search out areas of good practice or innovative suggestions and invite heads of department to present them to the rest of the group. This is a good way of trying to give at least some colleagues the opportunity to take away something of practical value from the meeting!

- Consider how to engender effective discussion and meaningful sharing of ideas. If you have a large gathering, consider dividing up into discussion groups before a plenary session. Consider the value of small working groups of interested HoDs, meeting separately between your full meetings, to explore an issue in real depth and report back to the main body.

- Be prepared to be strict about 'Any Other Business'. If there has been an opportunity to put items on to the agenda, you can legitimately refuse to extend the meeting to discuss something about which you have been given no warning. I've occasionally invited anyone who feels strongly about the issue to stay and discuss it with me, while allowing the majority who wish to leave to do so.

- Provide good quality refreshments! This shows that you value the time colleagues spend attending the meeting – and you may be able to smuggle something controversial past them while they are enjoying a cream cake!

Beyond formal meetings, it goes without saying that you will encourage your heads of department to approach you with any concerns they have – but don't forget to seek their good news as well. Some will regularly find their way to your door, or will pick up the phone. Others will need seeking out.

Making a point of being in the common room at busy times is important, even if you think you have better things to do. Getting out of the office and being a presence around the school is hugely valuable – when you can find the time to do it. Getting into classrooms to see teaching and learning in action is essential.

One major issue on the agenda for our schools is the new requirement for school self-evaluation, an expectation of the ISI inspections these days. In many schools the academic deputy is the member of the senior management team charged with preparation for the next inspection; this provides both a significant challenge and a major opportunity.

A number of schools have adopted the strategy of introducing in-house mini-inspections or department reviews, mirroring to some extent practice in the state sector. This can provide a formal framework for getting into departments, observing teaching and learning, and engaging with heads of department in discussion of standards and development planning in their area.

The key to the success of any such school self-evaluation process is the time to make it happen in a useful and practical way. In this context, is it wise to tie up your presumably skilled, knowledgeable, dynamic and (possibly!) highly paid academic deputy with some of the routine tasks that are often tied into the job?

A classic example of this is the arranging of cover for absent teachers. In many schools this is still a major task for the academic deputy. It allows you to get to know many of the teaching staff really well as they approach you with their requests and problems, to leap heroically into the breach to help out, or repeatedly to come up with a thousand and one good reasons why they can't possibly cover the allocated class.

There are two views on this question. One is that only a senior manager has the detailed knowledge and understanding of the teachers and the timetable, the sensitivity to the genuine needs and difficulties of colleagues, and the authority in the common room to make the system work.

Conversely, others feel (based on experience) that it is possible to find a non teacher capable of doing an excellent job, provided that they have the support and close involvement of the academic deputy – thus releasing one of the key figures in the school from an extremely laborious task.

Developing effective systems for using data to track, monitor and influence pupil progress is a major area of concern in its own right: so much so that a few schools have appointed a senior teacher (such as a director of learning) to develop this aspect of a school's work.

The academic deputy needs a very good understanding of the plethora of data available and a vision of how it can be used effectively to enhance teaching and learning. You don't necessarily need to be an expert on statistics or the technicalities of databases, provided that such expertise exists somewhere within the school that you can tap into and harness.

This may come from a non teacher recruited especially for this purpose or it may be led by a head of department or keen colleague who gets a buzz out of manipulating numbers. If you find somebody good, you will want to fight extremely hard to keep them! Sometimes the non-mathematical academic deputy has the advantage of being able to see the wood for the trees, and thus can prioritise the data to be used and explain its use clearly to a non-technical audience.

The best preparation for this part of the role is to attend one of the regular one- or two-day courses run by Durham University's CEM Centre at venues across the country. Recently it has started to provide events solely focused on the needs of independent schools, although the more general conferences also give insight into some excellent practice in the state sector.

One challenge in many of our schools lies in convincing colleagues of the usefulness of value added systems, such as MIDYIS, YELLIS and ALIS – not that these are precise or infallible methods of measuring progress, but they are the best available and they can fulfil a very valuable function.

Success lies in winning over a significant majority in the common room and embedding the use of the data in everyday discussion and practice. A well-planned and well-delivered INSET day can kick-start the process; this works well if it utilises real data from your school, and leads to practical outcomes, so that teachers can see a demonstration of the benefits of the data in use. You know you have made progress when, weeks or months later, you overhear some of the former sceptics discussing the MIDYIS score of a problem pupil in the common room!

Teachers use data if they understand it, have confidence in it and find it easy to access. Putting the files on the school network is a good start. Building value added scores into your collection of internal exam results and reporting systems is better still. Setting up efficient systems that will generate target sheets for pupils in key age groups – and training teachers in how to use them – takes you further still. Using value added analysis of your own internal assessments to identify underperformance, and to celebrate progress, ought to be intrinsic to the way we work.

At the same time you need to remember the systems are not foolproof: exceptions exist to every rule. The value added culture you create needs also to encourage teachers to use their professional judgement and expertise to question the data, and adapt or discard it in individual cases if necessary.

Meanwhile there is also ongoing curriculum development. The academic deputy has to be constantly on top of the latest education department proposals for reform in the world beyond the school itself. Change has been a constant in the profession for the past 20 years and shows no sign of diminishing.

Part of the role is to try to filter out the gimmicks and fads that appear today and disappear tomorrow without offering any real benefit for our pupils. As independent schools we enjoy a significant advantage in not having to blow with the latest wind if there are good reasons not to. At the same time we have to make sure we follow what might become a requirement because of government fiat, examination board specification or university admissions policy. Nor would we want to miss the genuinely beneficial initiative when it comes along.

With an increasing range of qualifications (IB, Pre-U, and IGCSE for example) and newly fashionable subjects (Mandarin, Well-Being and

Philanthropy being recent additions) on offer, we have the opportunity to diversify and develop our curriculum. It is to be hoped that this is always done for the best interests of our pupils, although we inevitably have to have an eye to what we think our parents will value – or put up with! We also have to find the skilled and enthusiastic teachers – not always easy, especially for schools located in less populated areas.

ICT poses its own particular challenges and opportunities. It can be a sink down which vast sums of money are poured – unless you have the staff to ensure that the systems function well, and that teachers are proficient in using it as a real aid to teaching and learning, rather than a mere toy. The academic deputy sometimes needs to be the sceptic-cum-critical-friend, asking: "What's the educational benefit?" But at other times, the role can demand that you be the messiah, pushing the pupils' entitlement to an ICT experience across the curriculum.

One of the joys of the position is having the power to encourage or initiate cooperation and cross-fertilisation between departments. In so many of our schools teaching is arranged in very traditional academic subject compartments. Yet there is overwhelming evidence that pupils also learn particularly well when these barriers are broken down, and if they can explore themes across different disciplines. Fortunately, at least in the pre-GCSE years, there is still space for enabling willing subject teachers to develop genuinely cross-curricular projects, perhaps via the medium of days or even weeks 'off timetable'.

One very topical theme is the development of independent learning. How often do teachers lament that their sixth formers seem incapable of taking the initiative or researching things for themselves? How often do we complain of a desire to be 'spoon fed'? Yet these are usually pupils who have grown up in our own schools. What do we do to develop the skills needed?

This is not merely a case of laying on study skills programmes – even though this is another important aspect of the curriculum for us to develop. We need to consider how to create opportunities for pupils to take responsibility for their own learning. This includes opportunities to fail, at least when that failure is not going to be a serious setback for them, and to learn from that failure. In the end the independent learner will achieve better examination results and go on to be a more successful university student.

For those of us who don't have a handy crystal ball from which to gain our curriculum insights, the best source of information and inspiration beyond the educational press is the annual IPD Academic Deputies Conference. Two days of listening to expert speakers is supplemented by the valuable informal opportunities to discuss common issues and to share concerns with colleagues dealing with them in similar schools across the country. Regional meetings, such as the recently re-established North East Directors of Studies group, can be equally helpful. Space to reflect and think about your own school in a conducive environment is hard to secure but periodically essential.

One further core task that needs to be organised effectively, and which can be very satisfying, is the provision of curriculum and options advice to parents and pupils. This often includes producing factual and descriptive booklets, organising information and advice evenings and individual consultations with parents and pupils.

Finally, there is the construction of the timetable. On one level this is a technical task that can be delegated; though many academic deputies believe it is a great asset if you can write it yourself. Computer programs and/or a willing timetabler can achieve a great deal but the essence of the timetabling process is a series of qualitative decisions, prioritising between rival claims.

At the very least the academic deputy has to be at the heart of this decision-making process, and has to be able to understand the nuances of the school timetable in depth and detail. Decisions need to have a clear educational rationale, rather than mere administrative convenience.

With all these challenges, there are a number of essential factors required for success. The relationship with the Head is crucial; without close support the role will be impossible. Alongside this comes enough time to do the job. Dedication goes a long way, but if the academic deputy is loaded with a large teaching commitment or overly burdened with routine tasks, it isn't enough.

Many of the difficulties can be overcome if an effective team is in place to provide the necessary back up. Access to reliable secretarial support is essential. A good management information system administrator can be invaluable, too. Efficient colleagues in charge of examinations, professional development and INSET, student teachers and NQTs, parents' evenings and cover are all a real bonus – but lucky indeed is the academic deputy who has all of these!

Ultimately, beyond the material resources, a sense of humour, patience and good listening skills are essential. A genuine interest in, and willingness to value, all areas of the curriculum are highly important, too. Above all you need a commitment to providing the best possible academic experience for the pupils in your care. Therein lies the essence of so much of what we do.

Chapter 5

The Pastoral Deputy

Charlotte Avery

Schools offer many different roles, rewards and challenges for teachers. Having had experience in both academic and pastoral fields, I firmly believe that good pastoral care must lie at the heart of any good school and that when undertaken well it is the most rewarding, practical and humane (if not the most cerebral) part of the education process.

I would assert that being a pastoral deputy requires more energy, quick-wittedness, flexibility and humour than its academic counterpart; the highs are higher and the lows are lower on this emotional rollercoaster. I would argue that the engagement and rewards are also greater.

If one is looking to become a Head, both academic and pastoral management are obviously necessary requisites, but a good stint equipping oneself with a variety of pastoral experience might well be the best preparation for Headship. Having sung the praises of this role, the intention for the rest of the chapter is to discuss a variety of models and challenges that might be encountered and to offer some strategies for approaching these.

As a pastoral deputy one spends one's time in negotiation with various interest groups which do not always share the same interests! The main groups are the staff – the Head, the pastoral team, teachers, pupils and parents. You will be constantly seeking the *via media* without too much compromise.

The best piece of advice I received when starting out as a pastoral deputy was to make up one's mind for one's self and then to stick by that decision; the point being that in all good dilemmas there is never a black and white answer, only shades of grey. You will find as many ways to skin the pastoral cat as there are people keen to offer their opinion and advice.

In brief, the Delphic Oracle's mantra, 'Know Thyself', is key: have an absolute sense of moral probity, and temper this with wisdom, fairness and a good dose of humour which will always be appreciated by teenagers. Avoid being or sounding pompous or prim: when chastising students it might be easy to fall into this approach, and at all costs avoid a hectoring tone when informing parents of their children's misdemeanours: in the main they are not stupid or unaware, and they are certainly paying the school fees!

There are as many different types of pastoral care structures as there are schools. Sometimes pastoral care is coupled with discipline and sometimes these responsibilities are delegated to different individuals. In boarding schools the pastoral structure is premised upon houses, housemasters and housemistresses and this is sometimes also the case in day schools which either have a part-boarding structure or which used to have boarding facilities.

In this model the pastoral structure is vertical (*ie* groups of students are grouped across year groups) and often strongly defined with housemasters /mistresses being the first port of call to parents, as opposed to other models where heads of year or heads of department might take on this key role.

More usually in day schools, girls' schools and the state sector, the pastoral structure is premised on the model of form tutors and heads of year which works in a horizontal manner, *ie* students of the same age being grouped together. In this model, the first point of contact with the parent is usually either the form tutor, head of year or in some cases, the head of department.

In the vertical pastoral model, the housemasters/mistresses quite often are the 'power house' of the school and can quite easily make or break deputies if they 'take agin' them. Some have been known to break a Headmaster or two over such contentious issues through deeply held loyalties as whether boarding houses should eat together or not, and whether there ought to be a commonality of dining hour.

These housemasters and housemistresses have actively elected to take on positions of pastoral responsibility as their *raison d'être*, to spend the predominant number of their waking hours undertaking this role and to give up much of their personal freedom for the greater good of their house during the term time: no wonder they feel possessive!

This brings a huge loyalty, passion and conviction, but also on occasion stubborn idiosyncrasy and a failure to cooperate or work as a whole school community, since the argument is that the loyalty is first and foremost to the house, not the school.

It is often the case that some housemasters/mistresses are quite simply better than others: some are naturally charismatic; born leaders; gods on the playing field and pitch; archetypically 'cool'; very funny and warm. Then there are the others, those who were once excellent but who have been worn out or down by it all; are irascible; simply don't care enough; were over-promoted when there was a dearth of better candidates.

Students know via the ever-pulsing beat of the jungle drum which is a cool house (read housemaster/mistress) and which one is the disaster to be avoided. In order to avoid elephant traps (read pushy parents), be clear what the school policy is regarding how students are allotted to houses. Is it by postcode? Siblings? Pupils from junior or prep schools already in the house? Be very careful indeed if you bend the allocation rule: thin ends of wedges come to mind. Better to be completely transparent and explain in good time; have the policy in writing and then stick to your guns!

If there is a very unequal balance between the good and the less good houses, decide how much damage limitation can be achieved through playing one of several strategies. If you, as pastoral deputy head, can utilise some of your pastoral magic to refashion a situation into better shape through energy, enthusiasm, flattery, humour and care so much the better.

Seek the strengths of each house, or draw on particular traditions in them. Is there any flexibility in the allocation of the tutoring role? Does the housemaster/mistress necessarily have to register a particular part of the house *and* take the PSHE session? See how much flexibility there is in allocating tutors to the houses.

Is there sufficient slack in the system for other teachers to take on day-to-day pastoral care while the housemaster/mistress has the oversight? As the adage says: balance in all things – so allocate tutors who have the above-mentioned star qualities to help out in houses where the leadership is weak.

Alternatively, or as well, ensure that strong students lead the houses. If you have some flexibility in *placing* students in houses, you might allocate several of the best over several years to houses which are perceived to be weaker, since students are as much influenced by their peers as their teachers, and good students will help counteract weaker staff.

How much is to be gained by having shared house meetings or year group assemblies? Be careful that this has the desired effect, *ie* to dilute the weaknesses as opposed to adding to the dissatisfaction by making the disparity yet more obvious! If things are truly dire, can staff be found a different role more suited to their capabilities than this key pastoral position? It is certainly worth raising any such issues with the Head at an appropriate moment...

The horizontal pastoral model has a different set of pitfalls around which to manoeuvre – including a sense that sometimes your team is not all that it might be because the tutors have basically found themselves allocated to your year group. You come across the attitude in certain teachers that they came into teaching to teach their subject and not to offer pastoral support.

Such an attitude manifests itself in particular guises: an openly grumpy reluctance to engage; a more passive/feeble "I haven't been trained/don't have the skills/time/experience to undertake this sort of work"; or the possibly more genuine "As an older/ younger male/female teacher I don't understand younger/older female/male pupils and certainly can't teach PSHE to them".

Again, specific qualities, such as the vision and energy to lead and inspire and the organisation and analytical ability to plan an effective, interesting and well-planned but flexible PSHE programme might help turn the disaffected. It is also worth insisting that PSHE sessions are observed by exactly the same method employed in your school for academic lessons, not only by you as deputy head for quality control but also by peer observation to encourage good practice.

Again, you need to be aware of how tutors are allocated to year groups.

Do they follow a group from year 7 up through to the end of year 11 or even 13 (a model common on the continent)? Do tutors stick with a group for a couple of years through a Key Stage, *ie* year 7 and 8, or year 8 and 9, 10 and 11, 12 and 13?

Are teachers given any say as to which year group they are allocated or is it done carefully (or in some cases, badly on a whim) by the Head? In this model, what about the quality of the year heads? Inevitably, as with housemasters/mistresses, some are more charismatic, engaged, fun, and reasonable than others.

Do the year heads move up with the year or do they stick and the pupils move? Are they on contracts for, let's say, five years, or are they permanently in post? It is worth discussing these points with your Head to see if there is any flexibility in altering the system if you deem this to be necessary. You will be in the best position to advise the Head about how such things are viewed at the chalk face. Since you will be leading this team, be as reflective and proactive as you need to be.

A guaranteed way to win the hearts and minds of your team, whichever way it is constituted, is to chair pastoral meetings with clarity and efficiency. As in any meeting, never ask for opinions if you have no intention of actually being consultative. So, establish with your Head what the boundaries of your responsibilities are and how far *you* can make decisions with the pastoral team.

There is nothing more demoralising for a deputy than agreeing a decision at middle management level only to find it contradicted and overturned at SMT level, and obviously nothing more irritating for the Head. Always keep the Head well briefed on any pastoral issues and get the steer as necessary *in advance*. Heads do not like surprises; nor do they like being bounced into decisions by over-enthusiastic deputies!

Always acknowledge, reward and thank. The ideal is to be well-tempered, and be over-generous rather than under-generous in your praise if it's a question of veering one way or the other.

Be well aware of what your brief as the pastoral deputy entails: is it simply pastoral care or is it discipline as well? Care and discipline are not always easy bed fellows and on occasion one can feel a bit schizophrenic, chastising a student one day for a heinous crime and then supporting him the next through a complex emotional struggle.

However, the two are so often linked and I have found it a most useful and rewarding combination of roles. If you are *not* the one to dole out discipline then it is (obviously) your duty to keep the appropriate person fully briefed on any pastoral care issues which well might adversely affect the behaviour of a particular student.

Every school will have a different model for rewards and sanctions. It might be worth reviewing yours to see whether it actively and appropriately meets the needs of students of the 21st century. Any good system will be appropriately graduated, and each step en route to praise or damnation will be clearly understood by both teachers and students. If you find yourself in a school that is changing its intake, you will need to plan very carefully for this.

In brief, younger children generally require more immediate goals and tangible rewards – waiting until the end of the year for an accolade at prize-giving can be a rather meaningless concept. Always aim to reward the good things, and have a culture that is positively looking for praise. A timely note of congratulation for exemplary behaviour or achievement across the board (sport, drama, music, academic prowess and charitable actions *etc*) works marvels with students regardless of age or sex.

As deputy head it will be your duty to review pastoral and behaviour policies annually. Keep these updated as regards child safeguarding and welfare; think proactively about *Every Child Matters* and about how the five strands of this policy can be actively embraced within the pastoral traditions and structures of your school context. Ensure that all staff (teaching and non-teaching) are updated as appropriate with regard to child protection issues.

Keeping children safe is now a major priority for schools and it is your responsibility as the pastoral deputy to ensure that procedures, policies and practices are well understood and followed actively and consistently by everyone. Remind the Head and the bursar of the necessity for key SMT members to undertake Safer Recruitment training and to ensure that CRB checks are in place for all staff.

Child protection awareness and training is something that simply has to be openly on the agenda, even if this is a new departure for your school. You will probably find yourself working closely with external bodies, so be proactive in this area and forge positive and personal links with your local police, LA and welfare services, including child protection officers.

You will certainly find yourself working alongside the school chaplain and/or counsellor and/or school nurse(s) so, again, it is worthwhile establishing a happy *modus operandi* with these key people. It might well be worth inviting them to attend housemaster/mistress meetings and/or head of year/year co-ordinator meetings in order to gain their (invariably useful) input into such areas as the PSHE programme.

A related issue that often falls under the remit of the pastoral deputy is the overview of the registration system. It is a legal requirement to keep an accurate record. It might be worth setting up an expectation that registration periods will be monitored and that inaccurate reporting will be followed up!

Alongside adult support networks, there will be student mentoring and support networks which are excellent opportunities to create the sort of active *communities* that we all wish our schools to be; these have the advantage of simultaneously offering opportunities for student *leadership*. There are many different models and all can work well, given the plethora of school philosophies.

Sometimes sixth formers and/or year 11 students are encouraged to mentor younger students, either offering a general service or being paired up individually. Some schools operate Big Sister/Little Sister schemes where the Big Sister is sometimes in the year ahead since she can remember very well what being the 'new girl' was like.

The most successful schemes are where the pastoral deputy, or another figure in the pastoral management system with enough clout, is actively backing the system. If you are not directly in charge, ensure that you put your weight behind that person who is.

If you are lucky enough to inherit a healthy school council, build on your successes by advertising all the good works that the council has achieved over the last few years. If the council is short on numbers and energy, spend time promoting the benefits of the council and use assembly time to discuss the rationale of such a body. Discuss the remit of the council with the Head and establish whether there is a budget available for the council. Try to negotiate one if there isn't one already.

Organise the council so that ideally the students chair the meeting and take the minutes – although you might chair it at first to show them how things are done. Explain to them the parameters of what the council is able to achieve: there is no point in the council getting carried away with asking for an Astroturf or swimming pool when your grounds and capital expenditure mean that these are wildly impossible dreams. Recording such ideas will only irritate the Head and demoralise the council if it perceives that they are nothing more than a talking shop.

Another important part of the role of pastoral deputy involves dealing with parents. One of the stressful issues for teachers is report-writing, where it falls in the year's cycle, how it fits with internal and external exams, how it dovetails with parents' evenings, public examination module results and with the ends of term.

As pastoral deputy with care for the teachers, proffer any advice on better organisation; the staff will thank you for any efforts expended on their behalf. Remember, too, what parents want: reporting which is both timely and honest.

Ways of skinning cats comes to mind again. Every school has a different reporting system. Are there written reports each term or is the practice to have parental contact once a term (which means a parents' evening and/or an At Home/social evening)? Do your reports go out at the end of term or is there a more flexible approach? How are reports monitored?

Do the SMT and/or heads of year take year group reports to read through and highlight the premier league, first and second divisions *etc*? If so, what sort of follow-up is in place? Do you as deputy head see the chatterers and poorly behaved and praise the good? If not you, who does this? Monitoring and target-setting is surely at the heart of what good schools do. It is a short-sighted pastoral deputy who would claim that such monitoring was not his/her responsibility, since behaviour and effort are absolutely integral to both academic and pastoral matters.

Do pupils have a chance to see their reports ahead of their parents and to discuss them with a housemaster/mistress or tutor? Do pupils set targets either on the report or elsewhere? Do parents have to sign the report to acknowledge receipt? Is there an opportunity for parents to respond, either via a slip or by an invitation to contact a particular teacher?

Does your school run interim grades between reports? What other monitoring systems exist: report cards and a detention system? At what point are parents contacted: is there a system that this is always done by email or phone or an interview? Who makes the initial contact: housemaster/mistress/or form tutor or head of year? At what point are you called in as deputy head?

At what point will the Head be informed about any pastoral issue? What powers have been delegated to you as pastoral deputy with regards to suspending and/or expelling pupils? The amount of responsibility delegated to a deputy often depends as much on the personality of the Head as the experience of the deputy.

Obviously you need the answers to all these questions in order to be absolutely clear yourself and to others about where responsibility lies. If you are caught up handling part of an investigation and another issue surfaces (inevitably issues are like buses: they come along in groups) then to whom are you going to delegate? The most effective systems are those where the parents and teachers are absolutely clear about who the point of contact is and what method to use.

Although the expectation as a pastoral deputy is that one is dealing with the pastoral care of *students*, you might well find that, unless there is a deputy in charge of staff welfare and CPD, an overview of staff matters falls under your remit. Be prepared to offer support against a background of issues, from young and inexperienced teachers finding classroom management challenging, to bereavement, stress, depression and illness.

The pastoral deputy's role is huge, multifarious, emotionally draining and time-consuming but it lies at the heart of any school worth its salt. Be proactive and reflective, think about alternative models for systems, consult widely and take decisions calmly. It is the most rewarding of roles

Chapter 6

The Senior Manager in a Boarding School

Carol Richards

I must confess to being a 'lifer': one of those rare breeds that seek to live and work in a boarding school. I have tried day schools, to be fair, and was privileged to work in an outstanding day school, yet I missed the 24/7 buzz of a boarding community. I live in all year round but I am happiest when the school is alive with the hustle and bustle of children. Don't get me wrong; I like my holidays, but to me an empty school is a desolate and soulless place.

Working in a boarding school is a 24/7 experience. You can't hide from it; it affords very little, if any, privacy, and if you are not careful you can become insular, forgetting that there is a big world out there and that, relatively speaking, most of the challenges you face don't compare with real world issues. Your 'house' or 'your school' can become an extension of your home and you can feel like it is a part of you. This can be both good and bad.

On the other hand, you don't have to waste time commuting; that important document that you left at home or in your office can easily be retrieved; you can meet with students or staff in a more relaxed setting after the issues of the day have washed over you. You have both the benefits of living in a community and the opportunity to retreat into your accommodation for a little personal time.

The approaches to the organisation of boarding can be quite different in different schools so, if you are contemplating moving between schools, take care not to make too many assumptions. I can remember my first appointment as a housemistress – it was to a sixth form house in a school where there had never been a housemistress before. I attended 'housemasters' meetings, supervised 'housemasters' detention and even wrote 'housemasters' reports for a time. The housemasters' meetings seemed to be the place where important decisions were made.

I went from that post to a job in a girls' school where the contrast could not have been greater. I found that the housemistress had a very different role and was seldom involved in discussions or decisions of a higher order.

In my current role as head of boarding, pastoral care and sixth form I tend to deal with more of the 'tricky stuff': the students who present challenging personal difficulties or behaviours. I have had an anorexic in every year of my 'boarding' career, and so you learn to be an educated amateur. However, in every cohort there may be one child who presents an issue that you have not encountered before. Pastoral leaders have to deal with the 'unexpected' quite a lot. What might have looked like a quiet day may end up as anything but, and what I have planned often has to be re-planned fast.

Managing the pastoral life of the school is very different from managing the academic life. Most staff are appointed to their academic roles, and their pastoral roles can be seen as an add-on. Academic middle managers (HoDs) can have stronger line management positions than pastoral middle managers (HoYs). Many teachers are comfortable in their classrooms but much less secure with the pastoral issues with which they might be faced. Teaching and learning lie at the centre of school life but when there is a behavioural issue, even in the classroom, some HoDs may be happy to leave it to the HoYs or house staff to resolve.

I discovered early on that children don't do things to bother *me*; they just do them because they are children – and that helped to de-personalise situations. However, disciplinary issues still baffle me on occasions, and I may play for time to decide what to do. It also doesn't hurt to let the miscreant stew for a time.

As with many boarding schools we have a large number of international students. There are the obvious linguistic issues and problems in communicating directly with parents, but there are also the cultural differences. A number of years ago the principal was visiting Hong Kong and invited the parents of current pupils to a buffet at her hotel, but few of them replied. When we investigated, we discovered that they would only reply if they were unable to come. Unlike people in the UK they all arrived at 7pm and left at 9pm, exactly as it said on the invitation.

A Nigerian parent was very friendly and would give me a big hug when we met, whereas an equally lovely Thai lady, with whom I had a good relationship, would always keep me at arm's length. A Japanese gentleman bowed, as is the custom in his country; I returned the gesture and then he did it again – which of us was meant to stop first? I invited a lovely parent from Pakistan for dinner and could not understand that she would not sit down: she believed that the guest should not sit before the host.

When communicating with overseas parents, how can we be sure the parents actually sent the emails and faxes we receive? I have seen a number that were of dubious origin. When we send a report home, do the parents ever get to know exactly what it says? For those people with limited English, do we choose the most appropriate vocabulary?

As the potential for misunderstanding is enormous, we need to act to mitigate against it. I try to ensure that all staff are given guidelines in dealing with international students, parents and agents. We are working to translate important information into a number of languages and we employ some native speakers.

The internet, computers, email, chat rooms, mobile phones and texting have brought great benefits, especially in giving students the chance to stay in close contact with home. Cyber bullying means that children can't escape the bully so easily. Staying in rooms playing with computers, DVDs and text messages does not help in developing social skills or integrating the community, and I would love to be able to activate a switch that made the girls' computers/phones all go off for periods of time!

Children can often phone home before the house staff are even aware of the issue. Last week we had a child phone home minutes after she had left a GSCE module exam that she hadn't found very easy. Within 15 minutes the parent was on the phone to the HoD wanting to know what he was going to 'do about it'.

Twenty-four hour news coverage helps us keep abreast of events across the world. 9/11 happened in the first ten days of my current post. I watched the tragedy unfold on TV while looking up contact information and timetables for our three American students, hoping that no one they knew and loved was caught up in it. When the tsunami hit Thailand over the Christmas holidays, I was left wondering if our Thai students were safe. More recently we had the devastating earthquake in China...

It is not just the news we need to keep up with, but also a sizeable amount of legislation and regulation that requires us to have an ever-increasing number of policies. How much does your policy document folder weigh in at, and is it available online? Do people read it? More importantly, do they follow it?

If a new member of staff finds that a child is drunk, is she going to search through the document folder or log on and find the policy file? I have reduced many of our welfare policies into policy briefs that summarise on one page 'what to do if'. We have put copies in each house, in the common room *etc* so they are easy to retrieve when needed.

People may not like procedures, but they do have to live with them. As educational visits co-ordinator, I live in hope that none of the hazards in risk assessments will come to pass. I also trust that, having acknowledged that they could happen and acted to mitigate against them, should disaster strike, we would be able to say with a clear conscience: "Yes, we did our best".

I have to deal with all the fire alarms and floods, the fireworks through the letterbox and the boilers that choose the coldest moment to quit working. My 'best' experience of this was when someone placed the tumble dryer on top of the washing machine. The washing machine decided it wanted to go for a stroll during its spin cycle. The tumble dryer however, wasn't in the mood for a walk, so as its base moved away, the tumble dryer tumbled happily into the water pipes. By the time I arrived on the scene we had our own indoor pool as we stood knee deep in water on the second floor, in about a foot on the first floor and about three inches on the ground floor.

As a result, I have discovered the importance of knowing where to find the mains water stop, the central heating controls and the power switches.

I have learned to keep in mind where the light switches are, and where the spare fire alarm keys and the replacement glass for fire alarm boxes are kept. When a fault in a smoke detector indicated a fire in a locked classroom, I realised how important it was to be able to have access to every key in the school.

Knowing how to rewind and then restart the CCTV is useful. Then there are all the door codes, the burglar alarm codes and the photocopier codes and, of course, these change frequently: it is a good idea to tell your partner if the codes change as it may cause him/her to go a little crazy when (s)he accidentally sets an alarm off at 5am on a Saturday!

These are examples of some of the myriad of issues that I deal with in my role as head of pastoral care, boarding and sixth form. For me, the transition from being a housemistress to taking a senior management role was quite a big step.

I would argue that the move from middle management to senior management is a bigger step than moving from being a teacher to a HoD. You have crossed the threshold between the staff and the management. You are sitting at a different table where highly confidential issues are discussed. You sometimes cannot explain exactly why that decision was made, and you may have to live with the 'flack' in the common room and know it will eventually die down. Under no circumstances should you dissent from the decision, leaving your SMT colleagues holding the baby.

You attend SMT meetings in two different capacities – in one as a representative of your area of responsibility, but in another as part of a cabinet, making collective decisions for the benefit of the school. In most cases the second responsibility overrides the first. You cannot demand for your boarding house to be decorated before some other area of the school that clearly needs to be decorated first.

I encountered a colleague some years back who would frequently remind people: "I'm senior management". I would advise against this; it is, and should be, a servant leadership role not a power trip – but that's not to say you shouldn't be assertive when necessary!

It took time to appreciate that other people are not like me! I may be a crazed workaholic, but other people are more balanced. I may judge commitment on time and energy expended, but shorter, more focused time might easily achieve the same ends, if not more. I might be ambitious, but other people are content with their lot. I might have a high level of initiative, whilst others may be happier to follow. Some people live in the moment, but I plan for the future. Some people like to stress only the good points, so it may appear to them that I overplay the devil's advocate.

To me the word 'consult' means asking what people think before I have decided what I am going to do, so that they might bring ideas to inform the decision. If I have made up my mind I am informing people. There are times for both.

A group of housemasters and housemistresses or heads of year attending a meeting does not constitute a 'team' – although over time and in the right conditions it may develop into one. I am an advocate of teams as I believe the benefits, in terms of decision making, understanding other perspectives, building group loyalty and synergy, are huge.

It is possible that the first few meetings of any group may feel like trying to get blood from a stone. Persevere, because it will work out in the end. However, don't have meetings just because they are scheduled on that day. If you have nothing important to discuss, cancel the meeting to show people that time is valuable.

I have learnt that silence does not often imply consent. "Yes" does not always mean agreement (let alone action) and in general "no" frequently means no. Some people have procrastination down to a fine art. My favourite response is "No, we couldn't do that, it is not our way"; I am obviously an alien.

If the first way does not work, I often try a different approach. At times, I accept responsibility even when I am not responsible, in order to save a loss of face. Sometimes, I consider that it is vital that I make a stand on an issue. However, the gains must be greater than the losses. Regularly, I try to ask myself: 'Am I doing things right or am I doing the right things right?' I appreciate that some issues really are complex – *eg* medical confidentiality within the environment of a boarding school.

I believe you need to have a good approach to managing your time and a sensible project management system. Anything that can be done in advance, should be. I tend to plan, to write lists. I don't fill up my diary as I know that every day will bring an unexpected issue, big or small. I know I may not get to the end of my 'to do' list, so I have to prioritise.

When I (rarely) get ahead, I go back to my lists and see what I can get on with. I worked with a Head a few years back who had a weekly appointment in her calendar. It was a two hour slot so that she could get ahead of her paperwork, but other people thought it was a meeting and so wouldn't disturb her.

We all need to create a 'work life balance' and in a 24/7 environment it is crucial for our own sanity to try to achieve it. When you are off duty, *be* off duty – in fact, go out, visit friends, go away for the weekend, drive down a long country road and forget about school, at least for a short while.

We need to make family time and appreciate that, for our children, living in a school is not a common way to grow up. My son, when he was about six, said to me, "I wish I were a boarder. I might see more of you then" – not good. My daughter once told a group of people that we lived in a big house with lots and lots of rooms and we had a swimming pool and tennis courts – if only. On another occasion she said that she had one brother and so many sisters she could not count them all – help, save me.

If I have made it appear that it is all bad, that was not my intent, for I have encountered hundreds of wonderful children and it has been a great honour to be a part of their journey. There is huge satisfaction when a 'demon' child becomes a solid citizen; when that anorexic who caused all that stress graduates from Oxford and thanks you for the difference you have made; when cards of thanks make you cry because they are so wonderful; when you get letters from past students telling of their success; when you get a mother's day card signed by every child in the house; when you watch colleagues whom you have guided and supported develop their careers; or when past students come back to visit as they did tonight.

Would I wish it to be different? In the round, not on your life.

'To love what you do, and feel that it matters – how can anything be more fun?'

Katharine Graham 1917-2001

Chapter 7

A Bursar's Perspective on the SMT

Gerald Ellison

For an SMT to be what it claims to be – a senior management team – all three words of its title must apply to its membership and be recognisable in its actions. Otherwise you will probably have a Head who (no matter how good) is neither using nor developing the skills of other senior staff to the school's best advantage. You will also have a management structure unlikely to be capable of meeting the demands of either development or disaster, or to help the school survive external scrutiny.

Each member of the SMT needs not only to recognise the individual skills and experience that the other members bring to the team, but also to develop an ability to understand their disciplines and to be willing to share collective responsibility. Members of the SMT cannot hide in their own professional comfort zones. There is a place for the procedural and, I hope, even in this legislated and legislative world, for the maverick. Which role is filled by which member of the SMT doesn't matter, so long as they work as a real team. Successful SMTs, like the schools their members serve and lead, are collegiate; they are what it says on the packet – senior management teams.

Heads and deputies are usually experienced educationalists; most have many additional skills. It is the *sine qua non* requirement of all non-teaching members of SMT to believe in the primacy of education in schools, to understand the nature of the world in which they operate, and to respect the abilities and experience of the educationalists with whom they work. There is, however, mutuality about this requirement. Most non-teaching members of SMT are also experienced professionals – often with longer, wider and more senior experience than its other members. Whether this comes from handling large and complex budgets, managing varied-skill teams, negotiating multi-faceted agreements, or devising and presenting or delivering projects, is immaterial: their experience needs to be recognised, used and blended with that of the educationalists.

Only then will you have a cohesive and effective team with which to lead the school. Never forget the advice that Harry Foot, a long-serving, former bursar of Charterhouse, used to give regularly to the HMC New Heads' Course. It went something along these lines: "Next time you dump a 'dirty' job on to your bursar because you can't be bothered with the detail of it, just remind yourself that in a past life, he or she may well have handled a budget and level of responsibility that you can only dream about."

Like the educationalists, senior support staff bring more than their specialist skills to the table. This can often be seen to best effect in handling people: whether individually or as a group; whether one's own staff or those of organisations with which the school has to deal; whether by leading, supporting, developing, disciplining or negotiating with them. No matter what their particular professional discipline, they are likely to have had considerable experience of managing a wide range of staff, projects and negotiations and through this to have gained that most transferable of skills – insight into human behaviour and its effect on the dynamics of organisations.

This may sound too good to be true – especially to those who have experienced insensitive, incompetent or simply ineffectual members of the support staff. There are occasionally bad bursars, as well as bad Heads, but in reality both are rare. Wonderful tales do the rounds at Heads' association conferences of procedure-bound bursars turning off the heating in April even though it is minus five degrees outside; refusing to replace plant and equipment that doesn't work because its replacement isn't in that year's plan; changing key codes, room numbers, telephone systems or parking arrangements without letting anyone know (or to any purpose); presenting budgets to governors or contracts of employment to staff that haven't been agreed or even discussed with the Head; or simply issuing peremptory memos. (My favourite ones tend to concern such weighty matters as restricting the amount of coffee or use of photocopiers in the common room.)

Just as popular, however, at bursars' gatherings are tales of maverick Heads creating new posts or awarding pay rises without any bursarial consultation or budgetary consideration, sacking staff ("he had to go") without even a nod to contractual process, or announcing to parents a brave new building project that hasn't been costed (let alone funded), and which requires the entire building development plan to be rewritten 24 hours before a governors' meeting and just after the bursar has sold the previous plan to the school's bankers. The tales from both sides are good fun, but that is what they are: tales that are fun to tell. They have no place in the running of a good school.

A good Head will be highly supportive and appreciative of the support staff. This extends to reminding the teaching staff at the start and end of term that most of the support staff – and certainly all of its senior members – have been/will be working, often flat out, during the school holidays as well as keeping up with the frenetic pace of term-time work. In return I remind support staff that the main purpose of schools is education, that it is the teaching staff who deliver it and that when the bursar is tucked up in bed with his cocoa, the Head and deputies are probably still ushering out the last guests from a parents' evening, *alumni* event or the lower remove drama competition.

The very term 'senior management team', although now ubiquitous, is relatively new in the long history of schools – historically, there was the Head and there were others. Among the senior staff the others might include a deputy (who in a large school might be more than one), a senior master or mistress and perhaps a director of studies. There were also bursars but they practised their arcane arts at a safe remove from the educational heart of the school.

Senior management teams, when they started to become established, included almost *ipso facto* the Head and the deputies – the senior educationalists in an educational organisation. For many years the most common models of a SMT excluded all others.

It is probably not much more than a decade ago that bursars became an unchallenged part of the SMT in most schools: you still see a few advertisements for a bursar that highlight – as if it were unusual – the fact that the role includes SMT membership. Since then the pace of change has been more rapid. Development directors and marketing directors, titles themselves previously unknown in schools, have been added to the team. Some ICT directors are included too but they are, as yet, in a minority. Human resources directors represent the latest growth area, but their title is usually a misnomer: on the whole they have a less than directorial role and are rarely SMT members.

Meanwhile the appointment of specialist staff throughout schools has also grown. Sports coaches, outward-bound leaders, special needs teachers and counsellors now fill many of the roles that only a few years ago would have been undertaken by generalist members of the common room with an interest in such areas. Among the support staff many larger schools now have a qualified accountant (increasingly a chief financial officer), in-house surveyor, facilities manager, or health and safety specialist.

Simultaneous with this growth has come the rise of consultants in the fields of occupational health, health and safety, PR, catering and marketing. Most schools now use more than one firm of lawyers (on a horses-for-courses basis) to cover charity, employment, construction and contract law, as well as the process of incorporation, intellectual property rights and the seemingly endless stream of policies. Even a medium-sized building project will have involved an architect, services consultants, structural consultant, cost consultant and planning supervisor. Some will have used a project manager. Many will have employed consultants on the Disability Discrimination Act and Asbestos Regulations and for rating valuations and planning advice. Increasingly, an external consultant is used to appraise senior staff (or to facilitate a governing board self-appraisal), or for curriculum and staffing reviews.

Specialist support roles have, of course, existed for a long time. Some such post-holders, like the medical officer, have been and are really retained consultants and are called in or referred to when the need arises and, usually, provide information for the SMT through the appropriate deputy; other established personnel, like the estates manager, accountant and the catering manager, although full-time members of staff, have tended and continue to report through the bursar.

All in all, it has been a period of change. So to take this chapter forward: *quo vadis* for the SMT and its non-teaching members? Which support posts should – or might – be brought into the SMT and which should not? What and how can the people holding those posts contribute to it?

Governors from the commercial world have a habit of making comparisons between schools and commercial organisations. It usually starts with a comment along the lines of "the Head is the chief executive" and continues (after a slight hesitation) with the observation that the bursar "is the finance director"; it then peters out as they wonder about those comparisons and struggle to find others. Fellows of collegiate universities are also prone to make comparisons between schools and their world – particularly when arguing for greater management representation on the board. The comparisons seem to me false: how many commercial organisations are governed by a board of non-executives? How many university colleges have non-executives on their board?

The acid-test for inclusion in the SMT is whether the role is directorial rather than middle-managerial or consultative. This is inevitably something of an oversimplification, but underpinning it is the absolute need, irrespective of every SMT member's individual responsibilities and disciplines, for them to work together. As in any successful corporate or collegiate organisation, each member bears some of the responsibility of (and for) the others, and, if the sum is not greater than its parts, the SMT is neither what it claims to be nor of great use. Let us now examine some roles one by one.

Despite the difficulty of finding someone with both ranges of skills required, the roles of development director and of marketing director are sometimes combined in one post. In other schools there are two people: one a director of development (or marketing) who also oversees the work of a senior marketing (or development) manager. Where the roles are distinct and equal (which is what is assumed below) there are crossovers, and it is important that clear responsibilities and good working relationships are established. How the responsibilities are distributed will depend both on the particular operational structure and needs of a school and also on the post-holders' primary abilities.

Assuming that the development director is responsible for *alumni* relations, 'friend raising' and fund raising, and that long-term success is likely to be measured by funds raised – through major campaigns, legacy campaigns and annual funds – this person needs to be party to the information available to the SMT and to be part of its corporate decisions. Without the intimate knowledge of strategy and policy and of the detail of a school's concerns, successes and failures that come from being part of the SMT, the development director's job cannot be done effectively. Whether development directors are talking to *alumni*, potential major donors, staff or parents, they must be authoritative about the school: otherwise no-one will listen to them and funds will not be raised. Put simply, they might as well not exist.

The same applies to marketing directors, whether or not the post carries with it responsibility for the admissions process. They too have responsibility for putting the school's message into the market place. Whether this involves carrying out demographic research and market surveys, placing advertisements, drafting 'brand-guidelines', drawing up prospectus or website designs, gaining coverage in the media, producing press releases, or overseeing all communications from the school, is immaterial. They must be 'in the know', otherwise what they put out about the school will be wrong (and therefore harmful) or (to prevent it being harmful) someone else will have to rewrite it – which means that they too might as well not exist.

While all good Heads, deputies and bursars have an instinct for and skills at fund raising and marketing, very few have sufficient knowledge of the mechanics of the respective disciplines or the time to practise them. Thus the presence of development and marketing specialists on the SMT also enables its other members to do their jobs more effectively – and to be spared oversight responsibility in these areas. Furthermore, the particular knowledge of this pair of some of the school's 'stakeholders' born out of the nature of their work, can bring a different and useful angle to discussions in the SMT.

Two final points on these two post-holders. First, although they are employed for their specialist skills, the good ones all have sufficient generalist skills to be able to work effectively in a collegiate environment. Those who do not will never carry the common room with them, and will make uncomfortable bedfellows in the SMT. Secondly, if you do not include them in SMT discussions, you are almost certainly encouraging them to develop offices and functions separate from the mainstream senior management of the school. This will both weaken the status and effectiveness of the SMT itself and can give rise, in the case of development, to the creation of a Foundation by default. It is far from unknown for Heads – and bursars – to exist uneasily between the contradictory ambitions of a governing body and a powerful fundraising foundation board.

ICT directors are important figures. They can contribute significantly to the work of the SMT, but they must truly be directors – with the breadth of vision and ability to take the whole school, multi-disciplinary approach that such a title requires, rather than simply managers of their particular corner. It doesn't matter whether or not they come from a teaching background, but they do need to be sympathetic to both educational and administrative needs, and to have a clear strategic view for the development of ICT that they can articulate to all types of staff.

If you do have such a person, in a world where ICT plays a part in almost every development (teaching and learning, administration, finance and, all importantly, communication), without which very few staff can function and of which every new building needs to take account, they will contribute materially to the SMT. If you don't, you will need to have someone else – a deputy or a bursar or a combination of the two (quite common) – who can assume directorial authority for ICT on the SMT. The latter, I would suggest, is better than having an ICT or network manager or HoD dressed up as an ICT director on the SMT, but it is still a second best option to the genuine article.

The reason, I suspect, that HR directors are not usually members of SMT is that their role is not the same as it is in commercial and other organisations – or, put better, it is covered effectively by other people. The traditional school model is that the Head (often through the staffing deputy) and the bursar (often through an assistant or deputy bursar) are responsible for the care and disposition respectively of teaching and support staff. Each selects and employs their own staff, and the bursar is mostly responsible for contractual and other legal matters relating to their employment, retirement or dismissal.

It is a system that works. Just because 'personnel issues' take hours of discussion for Head, deputy heads, bursar and assistant or deputy bursar, and because specialist legal advice increasingly needs to be taken over any decision, there is no reason for HR directors to be appointed to the SMT – unless Heads, bursars and their deputies wish to relinquish their higher responsibilities in this area. I doubt that they do and do not believe that they should. Schools, more than most other organisations, are all about their staff: they are collegiate.

Difficult professional or personal matters that need to be raised with staff cannot be palmed off to a specialist. You employ the staff; you support, encourage, promote and congratulate them; at times you also need to discipline and retire them. If it suits your organisation, then certainly employ a HR director or manager – but they are best used as specialist support to the school and its SMT (*ie* as sectional managers rather than directors, rather like directors of sport or catering managers).

We have now reached the point at which the role of the bursar needs to be considered in more detail – which forms the theme of the chapter which comes next.

Chapter 8

The Role of the Bursar in the SMT

Gerald Ellison

It will be evident from one section in chapter 7 that the relationship between the Head and the bursar is a crucial one. When the pair of them get on well and work well together, they bring complementary strengths to the enterprise, to the benefit of everyone. When they inhabit parallel empires, sometimes at opposite ends of the school (or, in one or two large and dispersed boarding establishments, at opposite ends of the town), condescending only occasionally to speak to each other, disaster threatens.

Fortunately, this latter situation is largely a thing of the past – although it might explain the old joke (dreamed up by a Head?) that 'bursars fall into three categories: fiddly-diddly, drinky-winky and naughty-naughty'. Bursars in their turn can be masters of black humour – as shown in a spoof glossary of terms in the *Bursar's Review* which included this pair of definitions:

> The words 'slightly overstated': term used by the Headmaster to excuse his earlier wildly optimistic forecast of pupil numbers.

> 'Understated': term used by the bursar to describe a budget for which he is responsible to the governors but which others have hugely and wantonly overspent.

There are many more like that. But in the modern world it is essential not only that the educational and financial arms of a school's management understand each other, but also that they are united in a common purpose. The previous chapter suggested that bursars can play a key role in the SMT in this respect. Newly appointed SMT members thus need a more detailed understanding than they may previously have had of the large variety of roles which a bursar actually carries out. The extent to which his/her work is delegated to others will, of course, depend to some extent on the size and wealth of the school.

The bursar has a large range of responsibilities. In most schools (s)he is responsible for finance (funding and financial planning, projection, reporting and control); buildings, facilities and estates (construction, operation and maintenance); human resources; health and safety (including security); catering, domestic and other support services; and legal matters (including adherence to statutory requirements). The job description often also includes risk management, emergency planning and disaster recovery. In smaller schools, where there are no appropriate other staff, it may also embrace development, marketing or ICT. All these areas involve important and time-consuming legal matters and general statutory compliance. In most schools bursars also serve as clerk to governors and/or company secretary; even where this is not so, they have a responsibility for supporting the mechanics of governance and advising governors.

HR, marketing, development and ICT have already been covered in the preceding chapter. The specialist nature of catering, facilities, estates, domestic and general support services involves comparatively little overlap with the roles of other SMT members (unless, for example, the school is serving less than healthy food or poor grounds management is having a negative impact on marketing). So let us concentrate on those areas which bring a bursar's work most closely into contact with the rest of the SMT.

Good financial planning is one of the key elements in a thriving school. All SMT members should have an understanding of the school's financial performance and the financial and regulatory constraints within which it operates. The bursar may have ultimate responsibility for the financial and fiscal well-being of the school, but successful budgets – *ie* those that meet both a school's needs and its expectations *and are achievable* cannot be put together by the bursar's department in isolation. Budgets should certainly be overseen and pulled together by the bursar and his/her team (do not forget that it is the bursar who presents the budget to the governing board and who stands or falls by its success). But successful budgets are only created through consultation and discussion within the SMT.

Aside from ICT – an ever-growing budgetary issue for all schools in a rapidly changing world – three of the largest areas of budget expenditure in schools are likely to be capital expenditure on buildings, teaching staff and other academic costs, and bursaries. It is worth us exploring these one by one.

First: finance and buildings (but concentrating on some aspects of financial planning and projection without going into any detail on funding or financial reporting and control). Capital expenditure is a large annual item in most schools' budgets. It is usually projected over at least a ten-year period – longer where a master-planning exercise for the development of buildings has been undertaken. Inevitably, where such large expenditure is concerned, not every desire can be met and priorities, consistent with the school's strategic and development plans, need to be agreed. While the strategic plan at its highest level will ultimately have been determined by the governing board, no effective board will have done so without considerable input from the school executive. More importantly in the context of this chapter the board will rely on the SMT both to reflect the strategy in its development plan and, through it, to deliver the strategy to which the board has put its name.

Nowhere is the delivery more *physically* evident than in capital expenditure on buildings. Although it will usually fall to the bursar and the bursary team to implement capital expenditure plans, the whole of the SMT needs to believe in the projects being undertaken and to help to 'sell' them to staff, parents and other interested parties. Its members cannot be expected to do this well unless they have contributed to the overall plans and have been involved in the creation of their detail. Furthermore, no matter how wonderful the architects and no matter how efficient the bursar, the plans are in practice unlikely to meet the real needs of the school unless the SMT has been involved.

Several years ago I heard a Head giving a talk about the design and construction of a new school. He suggested, almost as if it were a novel approach, that staff should be consulted on the design of new buildings. If it *was* indeed a novel approach – at least for him – I hope that by now it is universal. Consultation does not mean that everyone's wishes can be met, but it should mean that more wishes are met than otherwise would be, that the reasons why some wishes are not met are understood, and that fewer operationally impractical designs (architects are very good at these) see the light of day.

The old canard that consultation only leads to a raising of unrealisable expectations should be firmly squashed. However, for consultation to be successful, the management of the consultation process must be good. This requires the bursar and other members of the SMT to work closely together. They must all understand the rigorous timetable that is needed for the design, construction and commissioning of buildings to be on time, on budget and to specification. They must understand when discussion can take place and by when decisions have to be made, and must appreciate not only the overall financial constraints but the financial alternatives within them. They must above all have a clear view of the strategic and development plans and operational aims that the buildings are intended to serve.

Secondly: academic and teaching costs. Departmental budgets often cause the most rancour within a school – often, I suspect, because a bursar mistakenly seeks to control them on his/her own – and yet they are in many ways the simplest to determine. In terms of volume of expenditure, they are relatively small beer, and it is the academic deputy who has greatest knowledge of departmental needs. The bursar should set a broad financial framework for departmental budgets and allow the academic deputy to negotiate details with the HoDs.

The framework that the bursar provides should include not only a draft overall sum but also, in consultation with the deputy, a procedure for submitting and evaluating bids. If, following submission and discussion, the procedure needs adjusting or the overall sum is insufficient, the deputy and the bursar should together revisit both. Ideally, HoDs should be encouraged to submit a detailed budget for the coming year, together with at least an outline budget for a further four years. Not only does this encourage a longer term view, but if the expressed needs of a department cannot be met in the first year, it is more than likely that they can be met in a subsequent one.

The Head (often nowadays aided and abetted by the marketing director) will be most aware of prospective changes in pupil numbers as a whole (up or down). The staffing or the academic deputy will be most aware of exactly where staffing changes are likely to be needed to match this variance in numbers – or to respond to the expansion or contraction of particular subjects. The earlier that staffing changes can be determined, the easier it is both to budget for them and to bring them about – something which is particularly important in the unpleasant circumstances of having to reduce staff.

In the preparation of the staffing budget, provision needs to be made for pay rises and incremental drift, and there needs to be a contingency element for such things as long term illness, early retirement, extraordinary recruitment costs, changes to pension or NI contributions, or redundancy. These are all calculations that the bursar will make, but for many of them (s)he is wholly dependent on information from others in the SMT. Remember, too, the start of the earlier chapter in this volume about the staffing deputy: staff costs form a very high proportion of a school's expenditure.

Thirdly: bursaries, admissions issues and related pastoral matters. The pastoral deputy and the bursar often have knowledge of the family circumstances of a pupil that is better shared – albeit with proper discretion. The pastoral deputy may be worried about a pupil's bad social behaviour, poor academic performance, depression, tendency towards violence, and potential for self-harm or even suicide. The bursar may have related worries about one or other of the parents, or may suspect the cause of the pupil's worries through his/her dealings with the parents over fees or through bursary applications, or knowledge of divorce settlements, injunctions, restraint or other court orders.

Given these circumstances, it seems only sensible for the deputy to consult with the bursar before a significant pastoral decision is taken. Looked at the other way round, no bursar should take serious action against parents over failure to pay fees without checking whether there are known pastoral issues with the pupil or within the family. Even having checked that there are none, action should be taken only with the agreement of the Head.

In other circumstances – where, for example, a suspicion of abuse at home or drug taking arises – the bursar will need to be consulted on the correct procedures so as to ensure that pastoral needs, disciplinary action and the school's legal obligations work in concert rather than against each other. Anyone who has worked at a senior level in a school knows that all manner of human misery lies out there. The SMT in this, as in other matters, needs to share information and work together to ensure the best result.

Recent charity legislation has brought the award of bursaries much more into public view. Historically this issue has been the preserve of the bursar – sometimes working with a small team of governors who together constitute an awards committee. There are Heads who prefer to have no knowledge of which pupils are, or are not, bursary holders. There are also bursars who, despite interest from the Head, guard information about bursary holders as if they were one of the Secrets of Fatima. Such conscious ignorance and secrecy are well-intentioned – to avoid inadvertent discrimination on grounds of financial circumstances and to protect personal details. Both of these are very modern preoccupations, as well as representing traditional attitudes in independent schools. Total secrecy over bursaries within the SMT, albeit for the best of reasons, no longer serves schools or their pupils well.

On the bursar's side, information that comes from the detail of bursary application forms, and the related discussions that (s)he has had with parents, is also usefully shared within the SMT (as always, discreetly and only when necessary) when decisions on awards are being made. Most bursary decisions are difficult, as no two cases are identical and, no matter how detailed the policy that has been worked out, they usually require some subjective judgement with regard to individual circumstances.

It should be remembered, in choosing to offer a bursary to one applicant, that one is usually by default choosing not to offer a bursary to another. This situation, which will remain while there is a limit to bursary funding and no limit to bursary applicants, necessitates hard decisions which cannot be ducked. In reaching the right ones, schools rely heavily and properly on the bursar's analysis of a family's financial circumstances and his/her advice on financial limits, both to individual awards and of overall funding, as well as his/her usually considerable experience of dealing with bursaries and bursary families.

Schools also of course rely on the bursary policy that will have been approved by governors. But it is vital that these decisions are understood and supported by the whole SMT, whose members are often best placed in their interaction with parents and prospective parents to promote the school's bursary scheme. Some discussion, within the parameters set by the policy, is therefore essential.

The bursary policy of a school, its promotion in order to encourage applicants, and its funding to meet the demands of the applicants that it encourages are matters of high profile these days, as schools strive to counter reduced social mobility in the UK over recent decades – caused in part by the loss of Direct Grant schools and Assisted Places. The marketing director and the development director are critical to successful promotion and funding. They cannot, however, be successful unless they understand and believe in what they are promoting and funding. The best way of achieving this is for them to be involved in the creation and subsequent development of the policy. This is yet another reason, if one is needed, for their inclusion (see my earlier chapter) in SMT discussion.

The theme of consultation runs through everything. It is an unfortunate fact that not everything is affordable. One consequence of this is that bursars have a reputation (or are sometime best remembered) for saying "no". Both good and bad bursars will have to say "no" from time to time, but the good ones will have consulted closely before doing so. Really good bursars will also show how things can be afforded.

Some other issues: nowhere perhaps is the difference between nominal responsibility and actual responsibility more misunderstood than in health and safety. The bursar will usually be the nominated person responsible for health and safety in the school's formal documentation; indeed, (s)he may well be the person who has to answer for any breach of regulations, both to governors and in a court (although in the latter case, it is ultimately the governors/ directors/trustees who will be responsible).

However, every member of staff has responsibilities under health and safety regulations and they will (or should) be enshrined in schools' health and safety policies and guidance notes. An individual member of staff cannot act in defiance of, or contrary to, health and safety regulations and claim as a defence that it is the bursar's responsibility. An understanding of this should be central to the SMT's considerations. The bursar will provide legal and practical advice and take responsibility for the mechanics of health and safety management, but any material issues that arise concerning health and safety should be discussed within the SMT, and the whole team must be prepared to contribute to and agree the implementation of operational rules and procedures.

Risk management is something of a buzz term. It does not, as some persist in believing, refer to health and safety – although health and safety is included within it. It refers to all the risks – whether educational, economic, financial, logistical, legislative or demographic, or resource, PR or health and safety based – to which an organisation is prey. It requires that the risks are identified, measured, monitored, and where possible mitigated and controlled. It requires regular review in light of changing internal and external circumstances. It is an essential tool of both management and governance.

All guidance on the matter makes clear that this is ultimately a responsibility of governors. In practice, no matter how much governors are involved in the process, the risk management schedule is usually drawn up by the bursar. This makes sense as the bursar has a breadth of knowledge across the many disciplines and areas of activity that the schedule needs to cover, is concerned with both management and governance, and has the functional administrative skills and staff to pull the whole thing together.

For the risk management process and schedule to be effective, however, the bursar has to consult with other members of the SMT on the risks themselves and their measurement and control. Such consultation should not be limited to educational subjects: it should cover all areas. The draft document that is presented for discussion to governors needs to come with the imprimatur of the whole SMT.

Finally there is the relationship of the bursar to the governors. The bursar (whether or not clerk to governors, and whether responsible to them directly or through the Head) will have more contact with governors than most other members of the SMT. This situation is a simple consequence of the bursar's responsibilities, irrespective of his/her precise role. It has always been thus, but in many ways it is increasing. A significant amount of the time of most current bursars is taken up by matters of governance. As the process of governance comes under more and more scrutiny (the Higgs Report, the Smith Report, Charity Commission guidelines, *etc*) and as more school governors come from worlds in which issues of corporate governance are prominent, it is likely to increase still further.

The Head of course has a high level of interaction with governors, particularly the chairman. The Head and the bursar with the chairman of governors have traditionally been regarded as a triumvirate responsible for communication between those responsible for management on the one hand and governance on the other – and for the cohesion of strategy, policy and operation. Increasingly, development directors interact regularly with governors – especially where governors play an important part in fundraising campaign boards.

Alongside this development is a welcome increase in the involvement of other members of the SMT with governors, often through their attendance at meetings of governors' committees – for example, those dealing with educational and prep or pre-prep school matters. There is a good training role for deputies as members of the finance and general purposes or the estates committees: ideally once they become Heads themselves they will not be seeing the workings of these committees for the very first time. This interaction is good for governors too; it increases understanding, and improves the development of strategy and its delivery.

Care, however, needs to be taken in such circumstances that the SMT acts corporately. Good Heads and bursars have long recognised that if either of them acts wholly independently, without reference to the other, in discussions with governors, it is a sure sign of either an already fractured relationship or one that is about to break. A similar recognition needs to be present in all members of the SMT and the governing board. The principles of corporate or 'cabinet' responsibility should apply.

Ultimately, no member of the SMT (and, indeed, no governing body) can function effectively without the input of its other members. Both should represent a coming-together of complementary skills and experience. An open, collaborative and corporate approach is the only one that works, and all members of the SMT, whether teaching or non-teaching, need to leave their individual professional comfort zones and work together as a team. Governors, Head, deputies, bursar and other members of the SMT can all work to ensure that the whole becomes much greater than the sum of its parts.

Chapter 9

Managing the School in the Interim – Acting Headship

Thomas Packer

Per Aspera Ad Astra

Your chairman of governors has just asked you to take on the school. Your first reactions are a mixture of emotions: some very positive – it may just be the opportunity you have been waiting for – and others very daunting. You are at least one man down. There may be a major crisis which has sparked this adventure, and it will need to be solved as well as running the school.

At the outset there is a distinction to be made between a planned spell as acting head, such as when covering for a sabbatical, and taking over completely unplanned – perhaps the result of a sudden death or serious injury or maybe a disciplinary matter. The latter scenario poses many more difficulties, not least the public gaze. The press will always appear to know more about your school than you do, and it is vitally important that parents, pupils and staff hear the correct version of events before they read an inflated version in the media. But more about the media later.

I shall be writing about acting headship in a crisis. Much of the advice is appropriate, however, for a planned interregnum, the principal differences between the two being that, in the case of the latter, you have had time to think and plan ahead and you have in place a team that will be supporting you. In a crisis one has neither of these luxuries. In particular there is no one to do the jobs that you were doing yesterday and you may well have a restricted leadership team supporting you.

The first thing I did when appointed out of the blue at 8.30 one morning was to take assembly as usual. Then I sat in my study for an hour with the instruction that I was not to be disturbed (except in the event of a fire, bomb scare or pay rise!) to give myself time to think and to prioritise. It is only too easy to dream of one's own ambition, or to convince yourself that you can do everything on your own. That hour shaped the whole of my tenure as acting head.

Priority number one was communication. The media had been hounding the school for days, and parents were finding out about the school's difficulties from the local newspaper and not from us. This had to be put right immediately. Each day I would prepare a press release in conjunction with the chairman of governors; we would read it to the staff, and relevant parts were read out to pupils. Parents would receive a copy each evening in advance of it being published in the press. Thus they heard from us before anyone else. I cannot stress how important it is to make the press work *for* and not against you.

Priority number two was to restore confidence and balance. To some extent that was addressed through communication, but also through being seen to support the vulnerable elements of the school community and to insist on business as usual. Keeping everyone on task and focused. I drove the staff hard during this time, but balanced that pressure with love. The third priority was to establish a team that could pick up the deputy's duties quickly.

There is no time for training individuals to take on additional responsibilities; you need help now! Never make the mistake in thinking that you can go it alone. You cannot. You need colleagues who have a 'can do' mentality and whom you can trust and, incidentally, who will respond to that trust. I was particularly fortunate in having two individuals who stepped in and kept the ship on an even keel, more or less without asking and with no thought of additional remuneration. The head of maths (maths was my teaching subject) stoically arranged for all of my classes to be covered.

As I have intimated, business as usual was the key. With the students I made myself highly visible and made the standards of work and behaviour quite clear. I started by beefing up assemblies (something which I had been longing to do). I encouraged the head of religious education to establish a focus for each week that was introduced in the Monday assembly and followed up during the week in personal, social and moral education lessons and across the curriculum; the religious education, biology and English departments were particularly pro-active. Thus a whole-school focus on work and values was established.

Of course, when backs are to the wall troops rally round and my teaching colleagues were no exception. The solidarity of the staff and their determination to drive the school forward was exemplary. The mathematics department had to absorb my teaching, and the Head and the other members of the management team had lessons to be covered as well, so there was extra stress all round. It was important, though, to establish a focus on work and in a sense the extra load helped keep an air of busyness in school. I feared that underemployed idleness might breed a ghoulish enjoyment of the school's difficulties rather than addressing them, or at worst forgetting about them.

The parent body needed to be reassured that all was under control and that the school was moving forward. I had always been an active member of the Parent Teacher Association committee and this body was an ideal vehicle to help me. Our committee was composed of a mixture of highly positive parents who would do anything to help the school, together with those who felt that membership of the PTA brings with it the chance to have an involvement with the development of the school.

I suspect that most parent-teacher committees are similar. Both component parts have immense value in a crisis. I would consult with them regularly and always made sure that they were informed about initiatives and news just ahead of the parents generally. They were great ambassadors, both for me and for the school generally, communicating positively with parents and those outside the school as we clawed our way back to normality. Again the theme had to be business as usual; we went ahead with the annual ball, for example.

Of course, whilst you may have colleagues covering some of your deputy's duties, the crucial role of the deputy still exists. The 'jam in the sandwich' (as it is described elsewhere in this volume) is still a very necessary school ingredient even though it is minus the top slice of bread.

I continued to provide my 'Tom's Tea and Sympathy Sessions' throughout my spell as acting head. I also elected not to shift offices. These actions send out powerful messages to the staff and pupils about you, and it is important to get your own style over at the outset.

The first two weeks over, I began to really enjoy the experience. Here is an opportunity to see whether Headship is really for you; an opportunity, too, to put into place some of your own ideas. In my view, in the first few vital weeks, it is unwise to change too much too quickly, however enthusiastic you may be feeling; folk need stability in a crisis!

Which brings me to change. You have to ask yourself and your governors just how much change is advisable. If the present Head is returning at some point, he or she will not wish to see a school that is unrecognisable. Likewise a new incumbent will need to establish him or herself and must be given the chance to assess the school and introduce change at his or her own pace and with individual style. Indeed it is quite unreasonable to introduce change that shackles someone else. It is unwise to make major policy changes, curriculum changes, or changes to the pastoral structure.

On the other hand a re-timing of assembly or a tightening of the time wasted in the school day can go down well. Remember that as a deputy head you have a first rate view of what detail needs changing and where the school can grow in strength. Do not reverse the unpopular changes introduced by your predecessor last week or give in to a vociferous minority of common room. The easy trap to fall into is to see yourself as the complete opposite of your ex-Head. The reality is that the pendulum must swing to the middle, not the opposite side! Use this opportunity of addressing all the minor gremlins, capitalise on the school's strengths and identify and address the weaknesses.

In general, having moved on to Headship, I welcome taking on a school that has had an interregnum. Wise governors will see it that way as well. The rights are generally left alone by the acting head whilst the wrongs have been put right and who better than an experienced deputy to do just that? Of course you may have your eye on the Headship for yourself. In my experience deputies seldom make good Heads of their own schools.

Even if this is an option, remember that you will have to live with any changes you make. The whole business of managing change as an acting head is about reaching a balance between caution and progress.

The other aspect of acting headship is your relationships. You may have certain colleagues with whom you have a special relationship. That has to change immediately. As any Head will tell you, Headship is a lonely experience; popularity is a bonus, not a right! You will find colleagues who will come and see you to tell you "things you need to know". There are many hidden agendas and inertias in schools, and some staff will use a crisis and an interregnum to fuel their own particular ambitions.

The one body that you must trust and with which you must build up a positive and open relationship is your governing body. Its members are a part of the crisis as well. I spoke with my chairman daily for the first month, and everything I changed or moved forward had his and the governors' backing. Other areas of support came from the Association of School and College Leaders. Although you will not be a member of HMC or GSA, both organisations understand what you are going through and will be most helpful.

Don't forget your family relationships too. You are still doing the work of one and a half people at least; you are in a reactive climate as a result of the school's crisis and it is only too easy to become wrapped up in these demands and to overlook the crucial work-life balance that is doubly important in these circumstances.

As any Head will tell you, there are always minor crises that occur in the day-to-day routine. It is easy to allow those to dominate and cloud the real issue of managing a school in the interim – namely restoring and boosting confidence above all else. During my time I enjoyed my fair share of problems. For example, I encountered a suspected drug trafficking scare in the sixth form centre, and the school kitchens were condemned by heath and safety inspectors. The latter ran the risk of escalating into a major wobble; there are always parents who believe that the importance of the catering provision far outweighs that of providing a quality education. I learned very quickly that it is not the seriousness of the problem itself that is important; rather it is the perception of the problem and the subsequent action that is paramount in people's minds.

One aspect of acting headship never occurred to me until afterwards: the ramifications. When applying for my own Headship I discovered that news of the school's crisis had preceded me, and I found that some selection panels were convinced that I had had a hand in creating the crisis rather than solving it. At one school I was branded a liar because I had explained at interview how I had managed to keep the various balls in the air at once. The comment was made that I had claimed to be Head, deputy, bursar and chaplain all in one. However, there is no doubt in my mind that the whole experience left me stronger and gave me a better insight into Headship.

Throughout my career as a deputy head the time spent as acting head was undoubtedly the most rewarding. I loved every minute of it. It was easily my best experience of deputy headship, albeit for the worst possible reason. Acting headship is a great time to test out your ideas; you can convince yourself that Headship is – or is not – for you and you can visibly make a difference. I only experienced two hardships – keeping calm (which can be highly stressful!) and handing the school on to someone else...

Chapter 10

School Development Planning

Christopher Jeffery

School development plans have become such a normal part of the administrative furniture of schools these days that it is easy to forget that they are a relatively recent phenomenon.

For the first ten years of my teaching career it was difficult to ascertain, other than by implication, whether the SMTs of the schools that were foolish enough to employ me were following a discernible set of medium- or short-term objectives; it appeared that priorities would come and go as necessity dictated. As a relatively lowly member of the workforce I was not in a position to know of any coherent, holistic plan driving or dictating the issues that arose.

However, knowing the calibre of those who had the dubious privilege of leading me, I'm sure that they knew exactly where they were heading. The fact that I didn't is significant, and I will return to it shortly. Since then I have been responsible for the introduction of the idea of a fully consulted development planning process into two schools, the first as a deputy head, and the second as Head.

When the phrase did begin to appear in dispatches, it was used in an unmistakably distinctive context: buildings. For most, school development plans were all about new labs, girls' boarding houses, sports halls and theatres; space had to be chiselled out for development offices; and staff rooms somewhat suspiciously welcomed a new and very well-paid breed of colleague: the development director. Old boys and girls were no longer safe to enjoy the hard earned fruits of their school education without molestation!

As with many ideas in recent years – many of them valuable – a redefinition of the phrase 'school development plan' seemed to percolate in from the maintained sector. When Investors in People, ISI and other organisations began to expect such a document to exist, they began to exist. While some concocted a plan to ward off inspectors of various types, many more began to realise the great good sense – or even the necessity – of co-ordinating a school's planning, sharing it widely with staff, governors and parents, and prioritising resources in response. More recently still, the term 'school improvement plan' has also transferred across sectors, making the distinction from buildings-orientated development crystal clear.

Such planning is time-consuming and requires a significant degree of consultation, but has overwhelming benefits: in helping to prioritise the work of the school year and ensuring focused, manageable phases of a school's story; in ensuring that the whole range of a school's activities remains in the spotlight (for a Head, often caught up with particular strands of thought or pressing issues this can be vital); in targeting appraisal and staff training in a way that promotes the school's interests as well as those of the individuals involved. Above all, it draws together into a co-ordinated whole all the aspects of a school's work, and exposes any inconsistencies or contradictions in the total activity of organisations which are increasingly complex in a world of rapid change.It could be argued that the most important section of any school development plan is the statement of a school's aims that should preface it. Development planning cannot take place in isolation from these aims, and thus it should be possible to demonstrate that each strand of the development plan arises from – and is rooted in – them. The aims themselves will inevitably be somewhat generalised and, in the main, applicable to all schools, but there should be something about them that also makes them distinctively 'yours'; that reflects the strengths and emphasis of your particular school. In a world in which our marketing advisors encourage 'a distinctive market positioning', that shouldn't be too hard.

Starting the development planning process by revisiting those aims (to check that they fully reflect what the school is striving to achieve and to ensure that they do indeed speak of such distinctiveness) is, I would argue, a necessary preamble to the consultation process that will follow.

Looking at them together with the staff – including the leading support staff – will also act as a reminder of the purpose of the work that you all do ahead of the consultative phase, and encourage the sense of idealism that has to sit at the heart of that process.

Development plans imposed from the top, and those that grow simply from the mind of the SMT or the Head, are rarely if ever successful. The 'mushroom technique' (keep colleagues in the dark and throw 'dung' on them every now and again) doesn't have a great track record of success. A good plan, however, is similarly organic! It grows naturally out of the school's aims, strengths and needs as owned and understood by the staff as a whole. Any process of planning must give a voice to those who have to put it into practice and live with its consequences. But it must go further than that – in growing out of the collective wisdom and commitment of the common room, and, most likely, the key players among your support staff.

This can be achieved in a number of ways at the beginning of the planning process. Below is an example that has served me well at two schools.

Most teachers, at least at some point in their lives, were idealists; many retain such an approach. All, I would venture, entered teaching for reasons higher than personal gain (as if!), and most find satisfaction in more than their own intellectual stimulation. If there *is* not room in the teaching profession for idealism to play a central role, where *is* there room for it?

So – give the staff the opportunity to share briefly with each other what it was that attracted them to teaching in the first place, or what their best moment in teaching has been. This can have a remarkable effect by very quickly stripping away the everyday concerns that, all too often, serve only to narrow and restrict our vision, and by acting as a much needed refreshment in preparation for the task ahead ... a sort of intellectual sorbet, if you will!

Then set them a task that requires idealism, at least to start with. In small (carefully predetermined?) groups ask them to 'design' their ideal pupil at the age of 16 or 18. What would she have achieved? What values would he demonstrate? What attributes would mark her out? What else would he carry from school into the world with him, other than public exam success?

A similar outcome can be achieved by looking at the ideal school – an approach that might arguably encourage greater participation from the non-teaching staff. Bring the group back together to share their views and see what sort of consensus is achieved, but be strict in not allowing comments about "what things are like now" and "what prevents this from becoming reality" at this stage; encourage the ideal.

After a break for refreshment, ask the same groups the parallel question: what is our typical pupil like today? Encourage discussion about the most obvious areas of difference between the ideal and reality. Once these responses are fed back, my guess would be that a degree of consensus about the issues that affect a majority of your teaching staff will have emerged, be they curricular, pastoral, disciplinary, structural, or those most directly relating to school ethos and values. If this consensus doesn't reflect many of the existing priorities of the leadership team, something has to be done about the communication in the school, because leaders and those whom they purport to lead have lost touch with each other!

Don't be afraid to set some 'homework', especially if you are concerned that some of the less vocal staff might have been disenfranchised by the group approach. You need to be able to hear the sanity of the majority view clearly, and to ensure that it is not drowned out by the opinion formers and axe-grinders. The emphasis and range of staff opinion must never be allowed to get lost.

In my recent experience, carrying out the same exercise with the governors is a very good idea, both in giving them an 'emotional' stake in the development process, and in helping to ensure that they understand the core educational vision which should always be at the heart of any development plan. In some aspects of our planning, we have involved parental opinion too, and found that all the crucial constituencies – staff, leadership team, governors and parents – were thinking along the same lines. While an outcome like this can obviously give enormous credibility and momentum to a plan, you need to be confident that asking the questions in the first place is not going to produce answers so out of kilter with your own thinking that it creates an impossible tension.

Rather than talk in abstract terms about development planning, I offer a model of an effective development plan, but with a degree of trepidation. First, because the template that has served my two most recent schools well is a bowdlerised version of the ideas of two other colleagues. It originates in the work of Professor Brent Davies of the University of Hull, and Linda Ellison of the University of Nottingham, and can be found in their book *The New Strategic Direction and Development of the School* (2nd Edition: Routledge Falmer, 2003). There is much truth in their maxim that: 'Schools will not be able to continue to improve unless they move away from the over-concentration on the short-term and focus onto the strategic nature of planning and development.'

Secondly, I do not have experience of models adopted in other schools and thus am not writing from a position of breadth! And thirdly, the development plans created under the model offered have not been perfect, but that is a function of who created them, not of the theory they were based upon.

At the heart of the model offered, with its repeated emphasis on strategic thinking, is the idea that to restrict the vision of planning to five years, three years or one year ahead, ignores the fact that different aspects of a school's vision require different contexts. Davies and Ellison encourage plans to make a distinction between several layers of development and improvement at once, so that what might become important up to ten years hence is acknowledged in the document alongside that which is immediately important and pressing.

On the one hand there are those very big – even perhaps global – issues that are too nebulous or distant to make an immediate impact upon the strategic direction of a school, but nevertheless need to be understood and kept in view. Davies and Ellison label these Future Perspectives. They embrace issues as diverse as regional or national demographics and economics, long term sustainability, and transportation. These might be identified as those that might impinge on future planning, and they will need revisiting every time new information arises. As a rule of thumb, this section deals with things that might affect planning in seven to ten years time. We have a member of the leadership team who has a watching brief in each of these areas.

The second level Davies and Ellison call Strategic Intents. By this, they mean the identification of areas of school development that are believed to be likely or necessary in two to five years, but about which more clarity, information or understanding are needed before they can be included in detail in any immediate planning. In recent years, issues as diverse as new post-16 qualifications, changes to the university entrance system, the opening of a school nursery and the local travel plan have featured in our plan in this category.

The first of that list (ie new qualifications) has subsequently made it into the next (and arguably most important) category, Strategic Priorities. These are the three-year development priorities that should have been identified by the consultative decision-making process, and which will form the central thrust of the school's activity for the three-year life of this particular plan. Davies and Ellison would argue that planning *in detail* more than three years ahead is futile, as so much can change in the life of a school (for example, through internal changes and external pressures). Three-year priorities provide a helpful, realistic and 'graspable' timeframe.

If your experience is anything like ours, these priorities will cover the full spectrum of academic, extra-curricular, organisational, and property functions of the school, and will be rooted in the school's aims, as referred to above. Issues such as independent learning and curriculum development, improved school communication, behaviour management, staff terms and conditions, financial policies and the building of a junior school extension have been among those priorities that have been identified in the two plans I have worked on.

More immediate still, are the Annual Focusses. These are the specific targets or objectives, set for each academic year, that represent the steps to – or facets of – meeting the three-year strategic priorities. We set these out in a grid, relating each clearly to its appropriate priority, describing a desired outcome. We ensure that at least one member of staff is responsible for the delivery of each one, with a date for completion. In addition, we know that governors will want to be certain that the budget of the coming year makes provision for the outcomes to be achieved; some plans state specifically what the relevant sums are.

Having made the staff a central part of the formulation process, hopefully ensuring a strong sense of 'buy-in' to the eventual plan, it is crucial that they are kept involved. This can be difficult, particularly in the first year of a plan where there might be a lot of ground to be prepared or research undertaken, but it is nevertheless important.

There are various ways in which staff energy and activity can be bound in to the plan. First, working parties are a highly effective way of proceeding. Not only do they harness expertise among the staff, but they can be set up to be a consultative mechanism in their own right. Furthermore, staff with axes to grind, or those who can be snipers-in-chief among the staff body, can be transformed into the strongest allies when they are given the opportunity to exercise those opinions in a constructive body with a definite purpose.

Provided that the working groups know their terms of reference and understand the status of the final outcome of their deliberations, they can be immensely helpful. To illustrate, as part of year two of our current plan, we have five working parties looking at the following areas: post-16 qualifications; existing curriculum models in key stages 1-4; departmental monitoring; appraisal; and school website development. These groups between them involve approximately one-third of the teaching staff across both schools in the foundation, and are chaired by a variety of members of the SMT from both schools.

Secondly it is important to link the development aims into annual departmental development statements (and anything similar produced by other relevant and important constituencies within school). It is a good idea to require at least one departmental aim to reflect a key feature of the current stage of the school's overall three-year plan. Thirdly, it is worth considering making an element of the plan part of the focus of teacher appraisal and/or on-going lesson observation within departments (*eg* independent learning, the teaching of thinking skills or extra-curricular contribution).

One of the few things that is certain about life in a school is that nothing is certain! We all know that, in such a context, adherence to principles and standards combined with the willingness to be flexible around the detail of school life is crucial. The same is true of development plans.

If the plan – and its fulfilment – starts to provide rigidity and restriction to the extent that more immediate, and perhaps more important, issues cannot be dealt with as they deserve, it is not serving its overall purpose of taking the school forward in a measured and thoughtful fashion. Be prepared to be flexible on deadlines for the completion of a strand of the plan; what looked feasible in June may not seem so in February when boilers are blowing up, staff need recruiting in higher numbers than envisaged, or packs of irate parents are knocking down your door.

If items driven by three-year priorities slip a bit, it should be no big issue provided that both staff and governors are aware that this was part of the deal in the first place. Similarly, increased knowledge or experience of a particular issue may lead you to promote it or demote it in the order of priorities, or it may be necessary to transfer something from the Strategic Intents section of the plan into Strategic Priorities as circumstances change.

Will you always be successful? I would warrant that your plan won't achieve success in every regard; almost by definition a plan written three years in advance and containing the possibility for flexibility outlined above is going to be imperfect. Nonetheless, celebrate what you have achieved, or, at the very least, what you have put in place for future achievement. My governors found it very useful to have a clear commentary at the end of each year on which targets had been met, and why those that were missed had been missed.

I am also toying with another idea, as the end of our first three-year plan comes into view: that of a 'fallow year'. I am struck by the thought that those of us in leadership and management, who seek, rightly, constantly to improve our schools can underestimate the impact that supporting and coping with such change can have on colleagues who are already working flat out to do their best for their students under the existing structures. To have a year of no significant change and development is appealing; it enables us to address issues arising from the pace and pervasiveness of change, and to allow changes to bed-in. We could all do with time for breathing space.

Ultimately, as the pace of change in the world around us quickens, and as new initiatives are thrown at us or are available to us constantly, we need to ensure that we control, prioritise and direct the development and improvement of our schools to an increasing degree.

Chapter 11

Dealing with Complaints

Helen Wright

The acerbic American actress Lily Tomlin once said it was her belief that the only reason human beings developed language in the first place was because of their deep inner need to complain. At times it can most certainly feel like this to the senior manager in school; rarely are parents, pupils and the neighbour who lives at the end of the road (and whose peace has been disturbed by the fireworks on Bonfire Night) so eloquent as when they are complaining.

It is, of course, often the lot of the deputy head or other senior manager to deal with them, and sometimes we can be woefully unprepared. So much of our time in school is devoted to seeking to do the right thing, and making everything work for the sake of the pupils in our care – more often than not going the extra mile in the process – that we often, and quite naturally, overlook the need to develop, in advance, strategies for dealing with complaints. If we do things right, after all, what could go wrong? Parents, pupils and the wider public will all complain at some point, however, and it is a wise manager who is prepared for these situations and who knows, at least in principle, how to deal with them and how to prevent unnecessary escalation.

Trite though it may sound, complaints are nothing to be feared. All of us will have encountered stories of the 'parent from hell' – the difficult parent whose reputation precedes him or her, and who is rumoured to be entirely unrealistic in his/her assumptions of his/her child's potential and almost equally unreasonable in his/her expectations of what the school can, and should, do about it. These stories are, however, for the most part, exactly that – just stories or myths – and one of the most central strategies in developing a response to parental complaints is to realise this.

One of the most valuable lessons I learned as a relatively new Head was to appreciate that the parent whom I had dreaded meeting, fearing an inevitable confrontation, in fact only wanted the very best for her child, *and was quite right to do so*. Moreover, as I listened to what she had to say – how she felt that some of her daughter's teachers did not appreciate her daughter's particular needs – I could not help but agree that not only was it appropriate for her to want her child to be approached differently, but it was also right for us to make the necessary adjustments to provide it. We were not doing what we should have been doing; it was therefore entirely right for the parent to complain and for us to make changes.

It is a fiction that all parents have an inflated or unrealistic perception of their child's abilities: most of them have a very accurate sense of who their children are. Humour is an important tool in any organisation, and it can help keep us sane in school if we draw caricatures of outsiders, parents included. The moment we actually believe the humour, however, we run the risk of causing or aggravating problems which need not have existed. Parents are demanding – and quite rightly so, given that their children are the most precious parts of their lives, for whom they would do almost anything (including, in many cases, making huge financial sacrifices to send them to our schools). They want their children to make the most of themselves, they want them not to waste their lives, and they have the right to ask that we do all that we can do in the pursuit of this goal.

Educationalists rile at times at the notion of pupils or parents as 'customers', with schools as 'service providers', but we are precisely this. The transaction is a complex one, depending on many variables, most of them hidden or unknowable, connected with intelligences and emotions, and we can certainly never predict or promise a given outcome. Essentially, however, parents are sending their children to our schools so that they can grow into young adults with more knowledge, more understanding (of themselves, of others and of the world) and a greater ability to become successful human beings than had they stayed at home for their childhood and teenage years.

Understanding this is fundamental to developing a strategy for dealing with complaints in school. It is less a question of 'the customer being always right', as their analysis of the situation may be flawed, but certainly of adopting this approach: that if a parent complains, then something is wrong, and we must do something about it. I believe that something is *always* wrong if parents complain: either their complaint is justified and we must change something; or else they have misunderstood a situation and we have therefore failed to communicate properly and must put this right.

There will always be occasions when we make mistakes and fail to communicate adequately – in fact, there will be occasions when *whatever* we do, someone will not be happy. Recognising from the outset that we have the primary responsibility for resolving the situation will defuse the problem in a surprisingly high number of cases of parental complaint.

The greater the ownership of this 'customer-focused' approach by the whole staff the better. Regular reminders, INSETs and communication are essential. Leadership from the top is vital, and modelling by the SMT crucial. It is part of an empowering vision for a school – a desire to be the very best, to strive to provide the very best education and to respond to the needs of the pupils in our care.

All staff need to be aware that when parental complaints are heard and taken seriously, senior managers are not undermining staff, but rather they are engaging in this evaluative process. It is natural for staff – and for senior managers – to feel hurt and demoralised when criticisms are made; if, however, there is consistency and fairness in how complaints are dealt with, and an openness in exploring how they will be dealt with, together with confidentiality and sensitivity in the handling of actual cases, dents to morale can in most cases be quickly smoothed out.

Listening to a parent making a complaint is an art in itself. Speed of reply to the initial enquiry is of the essence, although this does not mean responding in writing to a complaint. The written word is generally an ineffective way to communicate (and can lay your words open to further misinterpretation, potentially exacerbating the situation). Phone back as soon as you can, or email to make a time when you can meet or speak on the phone.

Remember that in most cases, by the time the school is alerted to a complaint by a parent, this complaint has been festering for some time –

possibly even months – and for every minute that the school delays in replying, this festering is accentuated by the stress for the parent of not knowing how the school will respond. The Head may have asked you to contact a parent or you may have become aware of the issue; in any case, make sure that the Head is kept fully in the loop, as parents will often at some stage wish to speak to him/her, if only to be reassured that what you are saying has the Head's approval or agreement.

Holding the office of a senior manager does not automatically bestow upon the owner the ability to suppress all his or her natural instincts. We invest an enormous amount of ourselves in our work; we are generally proud of what we do; and most of us are motivated extremely powerfully by the desire to do what is right for our pupils. We are only human, and when a parent complains, we can be initially resistant to seeing that there might be grounds for a complaint in the first place.

If you think or feel this resistance, be warned! Our non-verbal signals are more powerful than we can imagine, and for any interview to be successful, we must be aware of the dangers and remember the customer focus. Listen, reassure, say you will investigate both the situation and what might be done about it, and promise to get back to them (and keep the promise). Use all your people skills to make complainants feel listened to, appreciated and special. In doing so you are in effect reminding them and reassuring them about why they chose the school in the first place – because it was the place where their daughter or son was going to get the best education and guidance. You are reminding them that you care about their child – and sometimes, this is all that it takes for a complaint to go away.

While the majority of causes of parental complaint can be dealt with by listening, by reassuring and by making simple adjustments, it is entirely feasible that a parent may wish something to change that cannot be changed, or may demand something that is really hard to fix in the short term. Inadequacy of buildings or grounds may be in your long term development plan, but this will have little immediate effect on a parent's ire, and the best you can do is to apologise and to seek to minimise the effects. Should you perhaps be hiring space at other sports facilities to provide access to an all-weather pitch for your top hockey teams? Could you look carefully at the timetabling of rooms to ensure that the youngest pupils do not have to move constantly between different classroom blocks in the dark, cold and wet?

Do not be afraid of embracing the issues behind the complaints and using them as a prompt for investigation and change. As long as all the changes you propose are linked back to your core values – and, if they are grounded in the wellbeing of the pupils in your care, they are likely to be – you may find that the complaint has led to a solution or an improvement which you had not previously considered.

Complaints relating to staff capability can be harder to deal with, partly because investigating the truth of the situation can be more difficult, but the same principles apply of listening, investigating and seeking a solution. In any issue which takes time, it is important to keep in contact with the parents and to reassure them that you are seeking a solution.

It is not a question of paying lip service to the search for a solution. If you have been able to embrace the complaint as a trigger for improvement (or, more likely, if you have your finger on the pulse, as a prompt to deal more vigorously with an existing situation of which you were already aware), then you will genuinely be looking for an answer to the problem, and you will be involving staff and pupils, including the parent's daughter or son, in this.

If parents seem to have a predilection for picking up the phone at the first sign of an issue developing, remember that in most cases they have been prompted, either deliberately or unwittingly, by their child. Children complain all the time – and if we look back to our own childhoods and teenage years, we can all remember just how often we felt things were unfair, or uncomfortable, or unjust. Complaining about these things made us feel better although, strange as it seemed at the time, it rarely seemed to have the same effect on our parents.

Remembering this with the advantage of many years of distance and wisdom allows us to be more forgiving of the pupils in our care. Children are always going to complain: it is a vital part of their exploration of their relationship with the world around them. Our role as educators is to help them to discover what they can do to accept or change their situation. It is probably fair to say that, whatever our religious orientation, most of us in schools adopt Reinhold Niebuhr's exhortation as we seek to encourage our pupils to acquire the 'serenity to accept the things they cannot change; courage to change the things they can; and wisdom to know the difference'.

A complaint by a pupil will not usually be solved by a philosophical lecture, however – although it is worth a try! Part of working out where they stand in the universe involves our pupils in questioning and criticising, being listened to, and being reasoned with, in the search for a solution. Nowhere is it more crucial that we model what we teach than in how we deal with them and with their issues. If we preach fairness and consistency then dismiss them out of hand or treat different people differently without explanation, we undermine the very moral messages that we spend most of our time delivering. Our pupils may – and often do – have a valid point to make when they complain, and the task of the senior manager is then to mediate with the other relevant parties, be they teachers or pupils, to find a resolution.

Complaints about behaviour of members of staff by pupils are particularly tricky. Serious complaints or child protection issues are rare but must be dealt with by the child protection officer and Head immediately and swiftly, according to the procedures set down, which may include suspension of the member of staff concerned. Less straightforward are complaints about teaching style: where does the boundary lie between what the teacher can reasonably be expected to do and what can be expected of the pupil?

Battle lines can be quickly drawn up. Remember that by the time a complaint reaches you, the pupils may have made up their minds, rightly or wrongly, about the intrinsic worth of the teacher, and attitudes can be hard to shift. In these cases, draw on as many areas of support as you can find: the head of department to talk with the member of staff (is there something wrong? Does he/she need support?); tutors and housemasters or housemistresses to talk with the pupils (are they behaving themselves appropriately? Do they realise what they need to do in order to get the most out of the classes?); and the pupils themselves. Listen to them and find out what is really the case. Most causes for complaint about teachers arise from a mismatch of expectation about how people should be treated or taught, and are often resolved simply through identifying this and finding a way to bridge the communications gap which has arisen.

Other complaints from pupils – about, for example, such issues (important to them) as the provision of toasters, the lunch queues and the range of activities on offer – can find a useful channel in school through the school council or house committees. These are only effective if a senior member of staff takes an active interest and is prepared to make things happen; this same senior manager can also quite usefully remind the pupils that with rights come responsibilities, and that the council has a duty to help create the solutions they seek: 'the courage to change the things they can'.

What of complaints from the public? In a sense, complaints from the wider public are easier to deal with, for most often they are either to be passed directly on to the Head, the bursar or the marketing manager. If it is a complaint about pupil behaviour, this can be addressed by the housemaster or housemistress; if it is a complaint about practicalities such as parking or noise, a visit from the bursar – depending on your bursar – might help resolve matters over a cup of tea. Vociferous complaints may need some action, possibly more local PR or community activity, but this sort of complaint is rarely as pointed as a complaint from one of your real stakeholders – parent or pupil. Again, however, exactly the same principles apply: listen, reassure, seek to solve.

If you are motivated at all stages by the desire to find a solution that meets the underlying need of the parent for his or her child to be looked after, in the vast majority of cases you will be able to resolve complaints without recourse to a formal procedure. In the process you will probably have helped to create a better relationship between the parent or pupil and the school. People need to feel listened to and cared for; if you can do this, you will have performed a vital function.

Keep notes of all your conversations, however, just in case, for you can never assume at the outset that a complaint will be resolved to the complainant's satisfaction. For whatever reason – including issues far beyond the control of the school – a parent may wish to take a complaint further, and will use the formal complaints policy of the school. You should be familiar with this policy, as should all staff.

A good complaints policy will have been drawn up with current guidance from the ISBA (Independent Schools' Bursars Association), and will contain timescales, appeal procedures and guidance for parents, Head and governors. If parents wish to proceed along this route, it will be in the hands of the Head, whom you will have kept up to speed with all aspects of the complaint and who will no doubt have been involved in helping to resolve it. If you have done all that you can do, let it go – realising that you have done your best.

Of course, it could all go completely wrong. If everything has gone pear-shaped; if the school is being sued for negligence, if solicitors are involved and you have had to call your union for advice, accept that you cannot solve every problem. If you have acted in good faith and have done all that you reasonably could do, kept everyone in the loop, and been motivated by the desire to do what is right and good, ultimately this will be recognised. Even if you have not done everything as perfectly as maybe you would have done in hindsight, do not torture yourself over it.

Most complaints do not in fact go to court, but in the intervening months when your Head is suffering from sleepless nights, when solicitors are playing drawn out games of cat-and-mouse and when your marketing manager is terrified of the potentially bad press, concentrate on managing yourself and reassuring yourself. You did your best, you have learned from the experience, and this was all that you could have done.

And when all the complaining is done, when you can sit back and reflect on the mill you have been through, the grey hairs you have acquired, and the furrows which have appeared in your brow, relax, have a glass of wine, and remember the words of Dale Carnegie, who, you may recall, was the author of *How to Win Friends and Influence People*: 'Any fool can criticise, condemn, and complain but it takes character and self control to be understanding and forgiving'. Enjoy the glow of knowing that you have that character and self control: well done!

Chapter 12

Managing Bereavement in School

Brenda Despontin

Whatever the literature available, whatever the courses offered, nothing quite prepares senior staff for dealing with bereavement in a school. Some tales are well-documented: Heads murdered at their school gates; teenagers gunned down by their peers in a rival gang; multiple fatalities on a school excursion. Mercifully I have no such tale to tell, my own experiences being more low-key, albeit equally as painful for those involved.

This chapter is therefore compiled in the knowledge that it is purely anecdotal, not based on any theory or recommended protocol, and that it can do little more than record personal reflections, with a few suggestions which might possibly help others.

Some Heads will sail through their years in post without experiencing the death of a pupil or colleague, but many will not, and the emotional roller-coaster which transports and consumes the entire community is difficult to anticipate or describe. But of one thing I am sure: the Head cannot face such events alone.

More than ever (s)he will need the support and wise counsel of the senior team. In my own experiences, it was invaluable knowing that we could allow each other some quiet 'time out' to grieve during the darkest days, covering for each other whilst ensuring the school continued to function. I was able to remain strong and calm in public chiefly because they were there, behind the scenes, propping me up in so many ways.

Inevitably, in any school community, there will regularly be individual cases of staff and pupils grieving for family members and friends.

Deputies, heads of year, house-parents, the chaplain and others need to be aware of the likely distress for the pupil or the colleague, and particularly if it is the first ever experience of grief. It is a complex, insidious emotion, not always easy to define or recognise, and one which can demonstrate its presence in physical as well as psychological symptoms. There are excellent courses for day and boarding staff which help them spot the symptoms, and having a matron or head of year on the staff who has had bereavement counselling experience can be helpful, as can outside help from associations such as Cruise.

In my experience, the worst family bereavements to deal with occur when there has been a suicide. I recall with great sadness still the tragic death of a boarder's brother, a university student. It came barely a year after their mother's death, and it fell to me to tell the girl the news. Needless to say, the boarding house was devastated, and the staff there were deeply affected by the incident. On another occasion, a day girl arrived in school having had breakfast with her father who shortly afterwards took his own life. Although her uncle came to my study to tell her the news, he froze when he saw her, and once again it was left for me to tell the girl. Who knows if I got it right? It was probably just as well that I had no time to think about it too much on either occasion.

Whole communities are affected when these tragedies occur, and every member of the SMT has a role to play in listening, supporting, and counselling. The most recent such occasion at my school involved a year 8 girl who decided to come into school the day after arriving home to find her father had committed suicide. My chaplain and her head of year comforted the girl whilst I spoke to the year group and my deputy ensured all the girl's teachers were aware of the circumstances.

The girl had asked specifically for school to be as normal as possible – but some of her friends were deeply upset, and needed to grieve too. Once again it was important for a team of staff to offer care and support for the girl, for her family, for the school community – and for each other. Never underestimate the emotional strain on Heads and deputies at such times, desperate to do what they can to help grieving pupils make sense of the situation, but juggling, as they must, the usual school business –

interviews, parents' evenings, concerts, governors' meetings – whilst carrying the deep personal sadness engendered by such trauma.

Time out when needed, a listening ear, and the love of a caring community will support grieving pupils and staff. In fact, it is often the bustle and routine of school which provides the welcome relief from a home destabilised by mourning, and a watching brief is often all that is required. The sensitivities of a good senior team help ensure that the balance is maintained between concern and what can so quickly be perceived as intrusion. Often, what a colleague most appreciates is flexibility over leave of absence in order to arrange the funeral and deal with all the business of death, perhaps at the other side of the country.

It is, however, a very different challenge for the senior team when death strikes a member within the community itself. In my 11 years as Head, this has happened three times, once unexpectedly and twice after colleagues endured a long period of ill health. The first involved a bright, popular sixth form leaver, killed in a car crash just days before A level results. As with most such traumatic events, I remember precisely what I was doing when I heard the news, away from school and in the middle of the August holidays. The girl's mother is a long-serving member of staff, and her brother attended our sibling school.

Conveying such news to others is not easy, but my pastoral deputy at the time (now a Head) shared with me that painful communication process, assisted by a few other staff who volunteered to spread the word. The girl's friends needed to be told, and her brother's friends and teachers. Parents and other pupils were informed by a letter from me, as were governors and former staff who knew her. My PA kept a check list, and my bursar and deputy met with me daily to ensure we had covered everyone. UCAS and her chosen university were excellent.

It was important to contact staff away on holiday at the time, and it was a time when answering machines and email came into their own. Our PR director composed a press release, and we vetoed any details of the girl's A level results. This was because local and national media sniffed a story, and we experienced some unpleasant tabloid tactics at the time, including a photographer hiding at the site of the accident to capture a shot of friends laying flowers.

A level results day needed careful management: the girls were still in shock. It was eerily quiet on the day, without the customary elation and noise, and there were many tears. My senior staff were outstanding, handling their own grief as much as the girls'. The whole school rallied to support the family in the days, weeks and months after the accident, and the funeral service included her friends' choir. My deputy and I both read at the service, and quite literally supported each other at times through that sad day.

Such sudden, inexplicable loss makes us all feel impotent, and it was crucially important to allow people to do something practical after term began. So the sixth form chose a painting for their common room, and the classics department worked with the family to plan a classics garden in the girl's honour. The stone for the ornate bird bath was supplied by the local quarry in the offices of which she was working for the summer. Occasionally, an old girl of that year-group still calls by to leave flowers at its base.

Can you ever be prepared for such an event? I doubt it, apart from ensuring that, as a Head, you have an excellent team you trust, and that you always have with you the phone numbers of all the senior team when you are away in holiday time. We also established after this tragedy a 'cascade' arrangement for Head and deputies, dividing phone details of all the heads of department between us, and asking each of *them* to be sure to have contact details of all in their department. We hoped this would speed up a contact system in any future emergency.

A few years after that tragedy, we lost a dear colleague after a lengthy illness. She had been many years at the school, her daughter had been a senior prefect and her youngest son was still at the boys' school. Theirs was a family well known in the community, and much loved. My chaplain was a great comfort to them, and especially the member of staff herself, who bravely decided to come home for her last weeks. Because we knew the prognosis, and because she had asked to see me to talk openly about her funeral *etc*, the senior team could, with the chaplain, plan for the inevitable. Those were grim meetings, but I knew that we would be better able to agree on the communication structure and arrangements without the emotions inevitable at the end. We planned what we would do if the call came during the day, in the evening, or at weekends.

When her husband rang, it was Mothering Sunday, and a raw date for me, as it was a year to the day after my own father's death. But I rang most of the teaching staff, assisted by my (current) deputy, leaving the bursar to contact the support teams. Staff were genuinely grateful for a chance to grieve privately that evening rather than be greeted by the news first thing on Monday morning. I told the girls in an assembly, then we set aside a candlelit room for quiet reflection, with the chaplain at hand and with tea and squash available along with a book of condolences. I told staff they could take time out as and when they wanted, that the senior team would cover for them, and we set about planning the funeral for the family.

The SMT kept busy, making sure school matters were addressed as normal, probably finding things to do that could actually have been left, but combating again that sense of powerlessness that pervades such times. I had not realised just how deeply we as school leaders would be affected too, nor how important it was to allow ourselves time to mourn. I still recall having to stop between meetings and phone calls in those first few days to walk outside and cry before dealing with the rest of the day's diary. I learned then that Heads and deputies need to be kind to themselves at such times in order to be strong for the rest of the community.

The funeral involved pupils, teaching and support staff. People again felt the almost physical need to do something practical, so service sheets were printed by resources, and our caterers provided refreshments in our dining room for the townspeople who attended. Later the staff forum designed and provided a staff memorial garden, close to the area where their colleague taught.

Within three years, it was happening again, as another much-loved long-serving colleague fell ill, and it became clear as the months passed that the prognosis was not good. Again, the senior team met with the chaplain to be sure we were ready for the worst when it happened. The member of staff in question had not wanted visits after a few months, but throughout the year of her illness, her colleagues and I wrote or phoned, sent postcards or emailed regularly, and I know that meant a great deal to her and to her daughters (both old girls). It was important to keep staff briefed about her progress, to keep her in our thoughts and prayers, and to be honest when parents asked about her.

She died just a few days before the start of the summer holidays. Again it was a weekend, and I was able to phone most of the staff myself, helped by my deputy. Again I told the girls in assembly, but the oldest pupils, who knew her well, had of course left. We were holding our leavers' service that Monday afternoon. Always an emotional occasion, it was particularly important to get it right this time, and my chaplain lit a candle at the start which burned throughout the service in memory of our colleague. My senior team and I made ourselves available for those leavers after the service, and provided a condolences book for them.

The funeral was held after term ended, so staff who had booked holidays could not attend. But enough girls from the choir were still around to sing at the service, and old girls came back from university to be there. Resources again supplied the service sheets, and I read a tribute at the request of the family, just as I had a few years earlier. Neither occasion was easy, but I know it mattered for those present, and felt right and proper to celebrate amongst friends that which had made our colleagues special and why we loved them.

When term started in the autumn, we held a memorial service in school, to which the family were invited. Staff who had been unable to attend the funeral felt they had thus a chance to say goodbye appropriately. After each staff death, to reduce unnecessary upset, senior colleagues quietly removed names from staff lists, website and pigeon holes, and colleagues in the respective departments arranged for personal possessions to be collected by the family. But the memorial garden remains.

Earlier in this collection of essays, Daphne West writes of the necessity for a Head to build a team which can take over effortlessly when the Head is unexpectedly called away. Never was this more evident to me than when I experienced my own personal bereavements, losing both parents quite suddenly, and within a couple of years of each other. I had not realised until then just how much there is to *do* after a death. Arranging a funeral whilst caring for a grieving elderly widow, herself not in good health, necessitated delegating to my senior team for a while, and I appreciated the subtle way in which issues just disappeared from my in-tray. Some I only learned of much, much later.

Staff, pupils and parents were wonderful on both occasions: I was touched deeply by their support and will never forget the chaplain accompanying me to the graveside each time, or the maintenance team helping to transport my mother's elderly friends to her funeral, or the card from a boarder: 'I know exactly how you feel and I am so, so sorry'. She had lost her own mother a few years beforehand.

Returning to work whilst grieving has its own challenges for a Head, and I was blessed with a PA and a senior team with finely-tuned antennae, who knew just when to leave me alone with a cup of tea. Heads get adept at sporting a mask when required, and I held up pretty well I think, but at one staff meeting the cracks began to show, and I apologised to those present. Returning to my study, I received a note from one of the older, wiser colleagues who wrote, 'Don't apologise. You're human too, and it's important for us to see you cry sometimes. This is how you give us permission to show our own humanity'.

I think it is a message worth heeding by senior staff when a school is in mourning for one of its own.

Chapter 13

Handling a Disciplinary Investigation

Nigel Richardson

Backseat drivers – metaphorical as well as real – don't have a particularly good reputation. The car driver doesn't normally welcome advice on gear changes and on why it would have been better to turn left two seconds ago. There is a similar reaction from the Head who overhears the common room know-all, sitting in his comfortable armchair and intoning: "I just can't understand why (s)he has been so feeble about X: he should have been expelled long ago". In both cases, things look much less straightforward when you are the one doing the driving.

By contrast, a truly supportive companion, map-reader, and conversationalist in the car can be immensely helpful, especially if the driver has a lot of other things on his mind. Again, the same applies to the Head, who will know all too well that dramas and crises often turn up in twos and threes, all too often when (s)he has a large number of more routine issues already in train.

And be in no doubt about it: high-stakes issues which may involve the dismissal or resignation of a member of staff or the suspension, required removal or expulsion of a pupil *are* stressful, even to a very experienced Head. Not only can they hi-jack one's entire life without warning for days on end, whatever else is going on at that moment, but they can also involve highly combative encounters with all the parties concerned. The stress levels may increase if the case goes to a governors' appeal, or if it attracts undue attention from parents or the press.

But surely these are issues which the Head is paid to take on, and which cannot ultimately be delegated – so why include them in a book about deputies? One (trite, but true) answer would be that we had no space for it in the earlier volume on Headship. Another might be that this book aims to prepare people for life at the top – and being able to visualise and anticipate how one should act in difficult situations is part of that training.

There are also three far more pertinent reasons. First, this type of issue reflects in its most acute form the distinctive role that the deputies should *always* be playing in supporting the Head. This requires a mixture of: "What role do you want me to play in this matter?", "Are you sure about the wisdom of what you've just proposed?" and "What other things can I take off you at this moment?" Put another way, it means the balance of remaining ultimately in a subordinate and supporting role, whilst also being a critical friend to the Head, providing the slightly more detached view of someone not in the immediate firing line.

Secondly, changing times mean changing balances of role. At one time matters of staff dismissal or pupil suspension and expulsion *would* have been matters largely left to the Head (and, in the case of a pupil, his or her housemaster or housemistress). The deputy might not have been involved at all until the whole affair had been determined – and then only so that he or she could act as the Head's eyes and ears amongst the common room backseat drivers. By contrast, nowadays, owing to a mixture of time pressures and legislative change, investigation has become more of a team exercise, with Head and deputies (as we shall see) playing complementary roles.

Thirdly, *any* deputy can be suddenly thrust into the hot-seat as a result of illness, absence on recruiting business abroad *etc.* School dramas don't (and can't) always wait until the Head gets back, either to rear their heads or to be resolved. Way back in 1989 I was enjoying my first weekend as an extremely green acting head while my then employer went off on a term-long sabbatical. At 35, I was very conscious that my normal post (second master) had always previously been held by retired and very experienced housemasters. I had never myself held that role, so I would be particularly on trial with the housemaster body.

On the Sunday afternoon a sixth-former on a final warning was caught in the pub yet again. At 4pm he was heard boasting to his friends that I wouldn't dare to send him on his way to what in sporting circles is known as the 'early bath'. At 6pm his parents arrived to meet me. I had to think fast – and there were two other weekends in that ten-week term as stand-in Head when I found myself making similarly tough decisions (yes: he *did* depart), as well as a major staff disciplinary issue.

Such issues come in all shapes and sizes, affecting all sorts of people – both employees and pupils, with an infinite variety of detailed circumstances surrounding them. So, can one size of advice possibly fit all? On one level, of course, no: but there are some general principles which will apply to nearly all such events and which I have found very helpful over the years, both as a deputy in two very different schools, and more recently as a Head. What follows is expressed largely within the context of pupil disciplinary situations, but many of the principles (and much of the practice) can also be applied to those involving staff.

Be sure that you fully understand the changed context in which we all now operate, compared with earlier times. While I guess it is easy for any of us to over-do the image of the all-seeing, all-powerful Head of yesteryear (defined by Anthony Sampson in his 1962 book *Anatomy of Britain* as: 'awesome and formidable men, whom no ex-public school boy can contemplate in tranquillity; wielding immense power … figures of massive integrity and moral uprightness…'), the modern Head operates in a very different climate.

The prevailing ethos of natural justice and the rights of the individual cannot, and should not, be ignored. In today's child-centred world we are all under far greater pressure to explain and justify our decisions. In the maintained sector there is far more of a tendency to require removal only as an absolute last resort. The exam system makes the risk of medium and even long-term disruptions to an education much greater, as coursework and module arrangements become more complex.

And – not to be forgotten – the young have a much greater and more sophisticated sense of fairness and injustice, and a healthy scepticism about hierarchies which haven't already earned their respect. Where teacher performance is concerned, all employers are now subject to much more stringent employment and contract law than was once the case.

Given all these things, don't be *over*-tempted to become a backseat driver yourself, especially if you start to feel that your Head is being pusillanimous. You may of course be right (*ie* (s)he is being just that!) – but remember too the old saying that 'The young have no fear'. That truism may be beneficial at times – especially if demonstrated by a vigorous new Head after a long reign in which things became a bit lax towards the end – but pursued to extremes it can also get you into deep water.

Some of us, towards the end of our careers, can look back on pupils whom we required to leave when we were much younger, and wonder whether we would be as tough as that nowadays. Remember, too, that many a Head sees disciplinary issues more tolerantly (equably? flexibly? *over*-flexibly?) once he or she has had teenage children, and has lived with all the judgements that adolescents sometimes get wrong. Perhaps the same attitude applies to those of us who have children in their 20s, when we have to deal with errant staff: I'm not sure. But the suspicion lingers...

With all this in mind, what follows is aimed to provide food-for-thought (and a check-list, of sorts), both for serving Heads and for those who see themselves in that role a year or two down the track. If at times it all seems rather dramatic, it should be emphasised at the outset that words such as 'suspect' and 'investigation' do not necessarily imply a combative and threatening atmosphere.

Remember too that investigation of major disciplinary issues involving either teachers or pupils represents only a comparatively infrequent part of a Head's job – albeit one of the most unpleasant and unavoidable ones. Handled well, long-term working and other relationships normally emerge comparatively intact from such events. Handled by bulls in china shops, the risks are rather higher – so know what you may be in for, and be prepared, as far as is possible, in advance.

So much for background and context. Remember above all that prevention is better than cure. Even the best schools cannot avoid the occasional drama: they come up with the ration to some extent – because places full of vibrant young people can never be wholly tidy unless they are also lacking in vigour and life. But there is a great deal that an institution can do *in advance* to minimise its risks if dramas do strike. If you have convinced the pupils that, as a management team, you actually like them; if you have fostered good links with the parent body and the local community (*in reality*, not just through slick PR); if you have the reputation for running a just and fair ship and admitting the occasional mistake; if you have won the full confidence of the governors; in times of challenge you will reap the rewards of accumulated goodwill.

People will be far more likely to trust your decisions, to accept your version of events; to assume the best rather than the worst. You will also need to be able to demonstrate that you have alerted pupils *and* staff periodically to the big behavioural pitfalls (*eg* drugs and bullying for the former: poor judgments over punishments and undue fraternising with sixth formers in the case of the latter).

This overall strategy includes having good written policies for pupils, and well thought-out staff handbooks and disciplinary procedures for staff, in place, and ensuring that they have been well written and legally checked. These should include details of how evidence-gathering and interviews may be carried out, the possibility of the need to segregate pupils and temporarily to remove mobile phones. They should also provide for good liaison where appropriate with parents/guardians and other agencies (*eg* police and social services).

There seems to be a huge number of policies these days, as the chapter by Richard Backhouse has already shown. The most relevant ones for this chapter include anti-bullying, alcohol, substance abuse and drugs-testing procedures, child protection, discipline *etc* – as well as grievance procedures for staff. The annual revisions can seem a time-consuming bore. But they will be an invaluable checklist as you steer your way through the various stages of a big issue, they will save time in the end, and they will protect you.

When drawing them up, expect to include lots of phrases of the *must expect to be* variety ('pupils who engage in X style of behaviour must expect the consequences to be Y'). This way you will have served fair warnings that there are things on which you will not compromise, but you won't be completely boxed in if unusually extenuating circumstances emerge late on in an investigation. Follow these policies to the letter if you can, so that people can't challenge you about discrepancies. Incidentally, a coherent behaviour policy will include advice on the difference between required removal and expulsion – something which is increasingly legally important in an age when what is on a pupil's record can be such a sensitive matter.

Senior management should not be afraid to take legal advice. New Heads are often very inexperienced in this area, and are afraid of spiralling legal costs. With legal expertise so much more specialised into certain areas and *pro bono* work more narrowly defined because of legal liability, the days of the all-purpose school solicitor who will offer no-cost initial advice (as well as being a governor: a frequent figure when I first became a Head) may well be a thing of the past.

On the other hand, while dealing with different solicitors for different issues can be more complicated, lawyers operate under a greater expectation that they will forewarn about likely costs – and be able to justify them later when the bill comes in. So, within reason, remember the maxim that spending money can sometimes save money. Don't be afraid to seek help if you need it, and don't hesitate to seek support and advice from a kindly and understanding bursar or an experienced chairman of governors on this matter.

The initial rumour or allegation surfaces. There is always an initial reaction along the lines of 'I could do without this just now' or 'Are we really sure that we want to pursue this question until we're sure that there is something in it?' Often, however, it can't be ducked. So the process of investigation begins. Much of the practical detail which follows is common sense, but be sure that you are basing your actions on certain well-accepted principles: reasonable behaviour as investigator; benefit of the doubt for the accused until the evidence becomes overwhelming; and not being both prosecutor and judge in the case.

At every stage, think calmly about what is best done by the Head, and what should be delegated to the deputy. Natural justice dictates that the Head cannot be both prosecutor and judge, and needs to be kept at a distance from the investigation itself; (s)he should *not* be the person who does the fact-gathering or initial interviewing. In the end he or she will be the one who will have to determine the outcome, acting in a quasi-judicial role and weighing up both the evidence itself and the appropriateness of possible outcomes.

It is important that interviewers write down details of meetings, or get 'suspects' to give written statements. Make sure that date, start and end times are recorded: if necessary, read over the main points to the person whom you have interviewed. Sometimes it is convenient to bring in a note taker. Get someone else to check for discrepancies.

In addition, take regular notes on the investigation itself – ideally in chronological form – at least once a day; if it is complex, designate one person to collate the material from all sources. Make sure that the bursar informs the school insurers if there is any risk of possible claims later on. Consider carefully with the chairman and/or the clerk to the governors which members of the board should be informed in full, which in outline and which not at all: those in the first category will automatically become unavailable to hear any appeal against the outcome (see later on in this chapter).

Early on, secure the evidence and keep it safe, so that no-one can claim later on that it has been tampered with. Isolate witnesses if you need to, so that there can be no prepared and agreed stories – but ensure that they are 'held' in reasonable comfort, even though it will be intensive in terms of staff supervision. Be extremely wary of insisting on personal searches, and take legal advice if necessary. Inform parents early on of possible difficulties ahead, but don't be pushed around over revealing too much too soon: you want to be fair.

Conduct interviews in a place away from the curious eyes of staff and pupils if you can. Carry out questioning carefully and fairly, warning those who you are about to question at the outset that while you are open-minded and will not be the final judge, the consequences of what you are investigating may be serious. Don't ask leading questions, even if time is short. Don't give hasty or rash promises of anonymity (which can be hard to sustain in practice, in small communities) or of an amnesty for those who turn Queen's Evidence. Be courteous and calm unless you are convinced that you are being wilfully obstructed, or that a little aggression may get to the heart of the matter – but if used, aggression must always be very controlled. Give regular breaks and, if necessary, meals and drinks.

Never interview people on a two-against-one basis: they should be allowed to *choose* a 'friend' (often a member of staff or trade union representative or a fellow pupil, who should be given every chance to speak and, if necessary, to consult privately with the person (s)he is supporting, although not to answer questions on that person's behalf). The management asking a suspect's housemaster to sit in on the questioning does NOT constitute a 'friend', nor does inviting one of the deputies to come in support of a member of staff – unless the interviewee has freely chosen that person. Consider enlisting the support of parents to extract information if you feel it may help – but make no promises, and (when you make this phone call) never underestimate the parental love which can cause disbelief in the face of the most overwhelming evidence.

Don't jump too quickly to conclusions, and be prepared to be patient. Pupils (and, occasionally, staff too) may have all sorts of conflicting loyalties. Adolescents face complex pressures from their contemporaries. However well-disposed they feel towards the school in 'normal' times, their instinct will be never to tell on their friends, unless they perceive that there have been actions which really are beyond the pale, or unless they feel that those friends really need adult help.

Resist the temptation to take the decisions which result from this too personally: even the best pupil tends to put his friends first. Remember how, when we were pupils, we resented the farewells that resulted when pupils were required to leave before their time. In investigations about illegal substances, be sensitive to the possibility that the suspect may have concerns about subsequent retribution from suppliers outside the school, if (s)he is thought to have co-operated with the authorities.

That same patience may need to be practised over several days. It is often well worth waiting to see what pupil gossip and rumour begins to filter through to staff – especially after a weekend when pupil mobile phones may well have been very active. Be prepared for an increasing amount of activity on social websites – and if appropriate see if you can persuade members of staff who may use such sites themselves at least to keep an eye on school-related activity there for you. You may also need to be patient with a queue of well-meaning staff and others who come to offer un-sought advice, or to make statements in support of the chief suspect. Don't be afraid to re-interview people, or to suggest to a pupil that gossip usually has a basis in fact, and a tendency to escalate.

There is, however, a reverse side to patience. All too often big disciplinary issues seem to emerge just before the end of a term (who was it who said that November can be the darkest month?). It is never ideal to leave an investigation half-completed over a school holiday. The school runs increased risks of tainted evidence, and it has little or no chance to control the un-thought-out actions and talk of pupils or parents who decide to weigh in themselves.

At such times, never make un-credible or idle threats – but you should point out to the person whom you are questioning that matters sometimes move out of a pupil's control if parents decide to go to the school, and outside the school's control if they take the law into their own hands and/or decide to go to the police: "This matter seems to be moving out of my sphere... With the holidays starting in a couple of days' time, I shall lose the ability to influence how other people see all this, and how they react. Are you better sorting it out with me, or with others, I wonder?"

Once you are satisfied as far as you can be that all the evidence has been collected, you should ask yourself some questions before presenting the evidence you have collected to the Head, so that the formal hearing can take place. Are further enquiries needed? Would an objective bystander consider the proceedings fair? What is the pupil's standing and disciplinary record within the school? What is the appropriate action or sanction, and who will need to be informed about it – and in what order? Procedurally, you would be wise to report the facts as far as possible without expressing a view either on the weight of evidence or the possible outcome, although you may of course be asked for a view.

What advice can one give to Heads about how to proceed at this point? Consider carefully what the outcomes are to be, and ensure that they are proportionate, both to the actions themselves and to the relative culpability of each individual. Take special circumstances into account, and don't be afraid to treat individuals differently, as long as you can defend your decisions later. Be prepared for the fact that deciding degrees of blame, and taking into account the previous track record of individuals, often make for what can *seem* to outsiders to be a very untidy or unjust outcome.

Never suspend a pupil without an immediate phone call to parents, and never require a pupil's removal without offering to meet the parent that day. Mark carefully my use of the words 'required removal'. It is wise for a Head always to try to persuade a parent voluntarily to withdraw a pupil, and to use expulsion as an absolute last resort: the former is less likely to have lasting consequences on an educational career, and nearly all teenagers deserve a second chance elsewhere.

But when you go into that parental meeting, steel yourself with resolve not to relent on your decision unless something quite new or unexpected emerges. In a day school, unless you absolutely have to leave things in limbo over a weekend, get things resolved on a Friday: it lessens the likelihood of fierce parental reaction on Monday. Keep staff informed as far and as early as you can about what is broadly going on – but don't be afraid to be firm with them, too, when they ask for merely salacious detail, or if your enquiries are not yet complete.

In an increasingly litigious age, there can be other pressures and demands, too. The public (and occasionally the police) may contact us deep into the holidays with complaints, allegations and demands for school investigation and action on pupils' misdemeanours. Parents, school supporters, even members of the public unconnected with the school, sometimes contact us for advice, or to warn us that something is afoot. Be very wary of being drawn into events over which you have no legal control or sanction.

On the other hand, don't be as naïve as our pupils sometimes are about the feasibility of a precise and tidy line being drawn between activity in, and out of, school. It is quite common for pupils worried about drug activity amongst their contemporaries to want to tip the school off – either to get it stopped, or in the hope that individuals can seek help. A major dispute between sixth formers outside school in the holidays all too frequently spills back into school once term begins. Once the school is told of drug activity, or one parent complains about the bullying behaviour of another, it can sometimes be very hard for the school to remain uninvolved.

In cases involving behaviour out of school, it is worth considering whether you should contact a parent to forewarn them that an allegation is being made. You can assure the complainant of anonymity, and you can emphasise to the parent whom you contact that you have no means of knowing whether or not there is any factual basis to what has been claimed. Most parents will be grateful for the information, and it is then up to them to decide whether or not to ask questions at home themselves.

Don't be too confident about catch-all statements in a prospectus about your right to protect the school's reputation though your disciplinary powers over behaviour outside the school term.

There is another pressure: the increasing use of parental threats to bring in the police, especially when allegations of pupil bullying are made. The police have a legal duty to investigate complaints made to them, but they are likely to be more enthusiastic about leaving such issues to the school in all but the most extreme cases. Pressures on police resources and manpower mean that their enquiries can be very protracted and often indeterminate. It is worth pointing this out to highly assertive parents, and asking them if they are *sure* that they really want to run the risk of 12-year-olds who have made unwise but off-the-cuff jibes about their friends being summoned to police stations for interview.

What about giving information to parents and the press? In cases of unusual drama – perhaps resulting in the departure of several pupils – it is generally best to be up-front with both. Parents like to feel that they are being kept in the information loop; most will praise your honesty; and it is better that they hear fact rather than rumour. The press mostly reacts in the same way (at local level, at least, where they rely on you for much of their 'normal' copy). But journalists also expect you to be straight with them, and those who live by the press can also die by it.

Most schools assiduously court press attention these days when they have good messages to impart, but they also have to expect press interest over things they are less keen to publicise. A story is more likely to die quickly if the key facts are volunteered all at once, than if the local paper senses some sort of cover-up. Never give, or confirm, the *names* of pupils in such circumstances.

In such crisis management, once again time and money can be well spent. A good marketing director or a media-trained deputy can take much pressure off a busy Head at such times, and while PR firms (especially in London) do not come cheap, the best ones can provide very valuable experience of crisis management. Don't be afraid to consult your professional association in such circumstances, or to seek help from ISC's press department. It is wise to keep both of them informed of events anyway, in case they receive press enquiries, or parents try to enlist their support against the school.

The Education Act (2002) requires all schools to have a policy on discipline and behaviour. This should include an appeal mechanism to governors in cases of required removal – with an appeal committee on which it is wise to include at least one outside member (*ie* **not** a governor). Some schools are now considering whether a majority, or even all, the members of such a group should be drawn from outside the governing body.

Either way, this group's total membership should comprise more people than will actually be needed on any given day, and it should be determined annually, when membership of more routine governors' committees is established. The outside member should be in place on a stand-by basis: you have too many other things to do in the heat of the crisis without having to find someone to play this role.

The parents of any pupil required to leave, and any teacher facing suspension or dismissal, should be informed of their appeal rights fully and fairly. Heads will wish to consult carefully with their chairman – or whichever governor (s)he has delegated to oversee the handling of the whole issue, if (s)he has decided to keep a distance in order to qualify to hear any appeal – about who should chair it and who should be called in to make up its other members. Be prepared for appeals to be made either on the grounds of flawed procedures or of an unreasonable decision, or both.

A good and sensitive appeal committee chairman is essential: an appeal well handled can do much to assuage the hurt feelings of all parties involved, and can often act as the tentative first stage in a healing process, even when an expulsion or dismissal is upheld. If, on the other hand, a new hearing is decided upon – which effectively reduces the previous enquiry to the status of a preliminary hearing – or the existing decision is completely overturned, different sorts of diplomatic skills and damage limitation will be needed to ensure both that the appellant slots back into the school with minimum fuss and that the Head (who, probably already stressed by the fact that (s)he is unused to having his decisions formally scrutinised in this way, will inevitably feel very undermined) is supported too. It *is* a lonely job at such times...

Finally, to return to where I began: the theme of staffroom back-seat drivers. They do not always appreciate our ongoing professional responsibility to the pupil trying to pick up the pieces of a career or an education. My own firm view about suspensions is that all pupils should be required to send daily packages of work back to school, and that staff should be required to set and mark it – especially where a fifth or sixth former has exams looming.

Where a pupil has to leave the school, it is sometimes (but not always) desirable for staff to go on setting and marking work, or even to teach a candidate privately. Good Heads will offer to support parents in finding another school. If they are wise, they will advise the parents to make the first approach *themselves* to a possible new school rather than asking the old one to do it for them; to consider a school not too close to the one their child is leaving (so that risks of mindless gossip between staff and pupils in the two schools are minimised), and to be frank to the possible new school about their child's misdemeanours.

Heads should also be honest in their dealings with any opposite number who contacts them to make enquiries about taking on the pupil. In the same way they will support a departing teacher in trying to find new work – at least to a degree consistent with child protection and other legal requirements.

For the driver at the centre of all these things, life can be immensely demanding and very lonely. Good teamwork from the other occupants of the car can be a great and sustaining source of comfort, as well as helping to ensure that the case is handled as well as the circumstances allow. In this, as in so many other aspects of school life, what was once a largely solo role for the Head now really has become a collective endeavour.

I am very grateful to Geraldine Elliott of Reynolds Porter Chamberlain LLP for her advice on the legal aspects of this chapter.

Chapter 14

Managing Special Events

Stephen Coyne

I thought it best to write this chapter based on my experience with one particular event at the King's School in Macclesfield: the visit of Her Majesty the Queen and HRH Prince Philip in 2002. I hope that some universal lessons will emerge during the course of it, and that a description of one particular event may appear more readable than an abstract collection of 'dos and don'ts'.

Whilst we all welcome important people to our schools fairly regularly, there are certain issues relating to royal visits that are probably unique. On the other hand, many of the issues which follow will apply to *any* high profile event in a school – not least the need for good planning beforehand, attention to detail, teamwork and clear objectives. And, as we all know, when detailed planning is important, the Head almost invariably turns to the deputy!

First of all, there was the bidding process. One forgets that we live in a politically divisive time! King's was about to be 500 years old in 2002 and we all felt that such a significant milestone might merit a royal visit. I was convinced that, were King's a museum or a university, this would almost follow a natural course. However, independent schools are hardly politically neutral these days, and I found myself having to put forward a case to the Cheshire Lieutenancy for the visit coming to the school rather than the town. I found this rather strange as the town was not actually celebrating any anniversary!

In retrospect, I think that the Lieutenancy was doing its homework and ensuring that it had all the arguments ready, in case someone might suggest that the Royal couple should come to the town in preference to the school. I found the advice of the local office to be invaluable all the way through this exercise: so much so that it has been the start of a splendid professional relationship.

Independent schools seem easy to deal with in comparison to local government and other organisations. There is one point of contact (who is not likely to move on in the next few months), and someone is in charge who can more or less dictate the way that the visit will be handled. Although our staff will not all be of the same political persuasion, the anti-monarchists in the common room are more inclined to ignore such an event than make protests. In general, that cannot be said for a local government organisation. However, in Macclesfield's case, the borough could not have been more enthusiastic about the matter.

I think it is also true to say that any single organisation with good-sized grounds is at a distinct advantage when it comes to the safe accommodation of a large number of very high profile VIPs. The obvious strength which a school has in this situation is security – the importance of which gathers strength as every year passes. Most of our schools have secure boundaries and can look after car parking, feeding policemen, potential hazards to people on the move and lots of other matters that are more difficult to arrange in a disparate organisation.

One should not forget the cobbles here in this respect! This is not a northern stereotype; I happened to remember from my previous experience down south that Her Majesty does not normally walk on cobbles or crazy paving. The local centre, outside the town hall, is on a slope and has some uneven paving – as I was quick to point out.

This exercise also made me reflect on the nature of the visit. The Lieutenancy is keen to provide maximum exposure for any Royal during a visit and it would have been easy only to concentrate on the school. We have always been proud of our involvement with the local community and the process of the bid made me think about the local organisations that we deal with regularly – so I ensured that I took them into account with the planning.

It is amazing how some things become set in stone early on, so this consultation was definitely a good thing. The idea of using the local Heritage Centre as part of our education display came out of this exercise after discussion within the SMT, and we might not have thought of it otherwise. On the other hand, showing off the school as the centre of the community is something we would all like to do, especially in the modern climate, and using it as the starting point and centre piece for any occasion is not a bad place to begin when picking up the first blank piece of paper.

Suffice it to say, our proposition was successful and plans for the visit went ahead with King's as the venue being confirmed. As already indicated, this does not mean that the bidding process was unnecessary; indeed, it was the most formative act in the whole process.

All the above events took place at least a year before the visit and it goes without saying that forward planning is a must for any significant event. Overtures to the Lieutenancy are well worth making up to two years in advance. Our Girls' Division is about to celebrate a significant milestone in two years' time and we are already putting plans together.

I have had a preliminary telephone conversation with the Lieutenancy to test the water and they have advised putting a proposal together now. This all helps with their planning and the key point is that they know which Royals will be in the area and when. It is not coincidence that several events take place on one day. It is all part of good planning, and notification cannot really come too early.

Next there was the planning of the visit itself. The school effectively celebrated its birthday on 25th January that year and that was the date suggested for the visit in the first place. We were actually assigned 24th July which (I am sure you will have realised) is a couple of weeks into the school holidays. The Royal party was involved in another high profile event in Manchester the following day, and this was the logic behind the date. On several occasions during the year, I found myself swallowing hard and just smiling in agreement. In the end, one cannot really say that the arrangements are not convenient. Since when do Head Teachers need a summer holiday anyway?

One of the major issues relating to this type of event is that it needs to be kept secret until approval is given. However, the basic format of the visit needs confirming before the original approval is granted. This produced lots of conspiratorial conversations where plans were considered and members of the SMT were delegated to sound people out on a whole variety of issues. We took the view that everyone would be delighted to be involved, and we agreed dramatic and musical events long before we had ever spoken to a musician or a thespian.

We had no alternative to doing this, but it was a bit of a worry at the time. One also has to take preferences into account: for instance, Prince Philip is keen on the outdoors and the military, whereas the Queen is more inclined towards the arts and history. We saw this as an opportunity rather than a problem, and we produced separate programmes for each of them and Her Majesty was guided by me and a governor chaperoned the Prince.

There are certain perennial issues that crop up at this point. Unveiling foundation stones, buildings and plaques are bread-and-butter tasks for a Royal; they also ensure that there is a permanent record of the event for future generations. This is also a good opportunity to lay out the school's priorities. I am sure that we all value our music and drama but we also wanted to show off our sailing club and outdoor pursuits. Each school will know best what its priorities are, but it is worth remembering that whatever happens will get a lot of publicity, and will shape the school's image in the local environment for many years to come.

Having kept the whole thing quiet for a suitable length of time, we then had to deal with the actual announcement of the event. There was much discussion with the SMT about how best to publicise the news once it broke. We decided to tell people at school through our normal briefing channels. Declaring that there is to be a special announcement in 24 hours' time is a good way to get the rumour machine working overtime and to create maximum anticipation, but it also has a down-side: we were busy enough already without having to spend lots of time answering questions about uninformed speculation.

We also had to be ready to place the information with the press, embargoed until exactly the same time as we were making the announcement within the school. Our local newspaper goes to press on Wednesday and we announced the visit on the Monday, via our press officer, to ensure that the paper had time to include it. Any later might have meant it getting poor coverage, and it would have looked like old news had we declared before the weekend and then allowed several days to elapse before the press could include it.

Typically, the newspapers always want more information than you can give them. Our press release told them some of the things that the Royal couple would do, without committing us to too much detail. The programme did change as time went by, but our original release proved still to be accurate, even after the visit was completed. One other thing proved to be right: arguing that the event was a coup for the whole community (and not just for King's) seemed to be a good piece of public relations.

Having managed to secure the event at the school, there was still the issue of the county and the borough to be considered. This event was the only significant royal visit to Cheshire during that year. As such, there was a strong feeling in the borough and the county that the visitors should see what was on offer throughout the area.

We agreed that, while the visit to King's would last an hour, the couple would spend 15 minutes in the building touring the school and then 45 minutes on the front field seeing the best of Cheshire. This may not seem generous to the school, but what we got was effectively 30 minutes because we had two programmes to put together. I can assure anyone involved in such an event that half-an-hour is plenty of time; there is no need to look for more!

As a result of this arrangement, I was involved in regular meetings for a whole year with the chief executive of Macclesfield, the Lieutenancy and local press people. One of the main decisions was what type of gift to present to the Royal couple, and how it would represent the different parts of the county. Eventually, it was decided to produce a map made of silk, showing the different parts of the area.

The central section showed the school. This was not our suggestion, but it found favour with the community and we were delighted. I managed to invoke derision at one of the meetings by insisting that the school's name should contain an apostrophe! It is amazing how the outside world considers this kind of thing to be pedantic in the extreme, whereas we would all agree that it is simply a matter of getting things right.

The next stage was to confirm the programme. Although this had been agreed in outline at the very start of the proposal, the detail continued to evolve until the final few weeks. We had a theme based upon education in 1502 (our year of foundation), 1952 (the Coronation year) and education in the future. Some ICT companies offered to help us with the futuristic area, and one of the SMT did all the negotiation with them so that the concept constantly developed.

We were persuaded beforehand that Her Majesty was less keen on technology than history. However, from her comments after the event, she was obviously very impressed with the ICT suite, but did not have much to say about the short historical drama. So much for all the advance planning!

The SMT and I drew up a very careful timescale for each part of the programme, allocating the precise number of minutes that would elapse at each venue. We timed the performance and events to the second, as well as walking from place to place with a watch to make sure our estimate was accurate. In this way we ensured we could run to time. Sometimes finishing early is as bad as being late if events follow on from each other – especially if the start of one item is dependent on the completion of a previous one. Having such a timeline is a must for a major occasion.

Living in the wet north-west, we also had to have wet and dry weather schedules. These had to be similar enough for an easy transition between the two should a decision about which programme was running be required late in the day. We also agreed a deadline by which this decision should be taken. The weather forecast can sometimes be helpful but it was not to us! In the end, we played safe, going for the wet weather programme. At that stage, we were well past worrying about the options; we just wanted a decision. As things eventually turned out, we had a typical summer day in Macclesfield with steel grey skies and a cold afternoon but at least it was not actually raining.

To what extent did the visit promote the school? We have never had a story that ran and ran for us with the local papers in the way that this one did. We gave regular updates and made reference to the visit in almost every other story we wrote for the papers that year – and the year after.

We invited all our neighbours whose homes actually border the school to the grounds for the hour of the visit. After all, they regularly tolerate our school buses crowded with teenagers. It was wonderful to read in the papers that the school had been so generous, and that the pupils 'do not cause us any problems and are always well behaved'. Fortunately, journalists have never read my postbag on such matters! The ticket arrangements were very complex and we were limited to 1000 people on site for health and safety reasons, but the actual uptake by neighbours was relatively low because it was a working day.

This brings me to one of the other issues we faced. Who precisely was welcoming our guests? We knew who was dealing with the two central figures, but what about our governors, feeder school Heads *etc*? As a result of our experience of this event, for all major school functions we now have a reception list. Every member of the SMT is allocated people to host. They do not have to stay with them all the time, although that might be how things turn out, but they do have to greet them and introduce them to like-minded parties. This avoids guests being left or feeling overlooked. It would have been very easy for such an outcome to occur under the pressures we had on that day; fortunately for us, we successfully avoided it.

We also allocated differently coloured tickets. Governors, parents, members of the choir and others were denoted by different hues, and that definitely helped speedily to identify people. It was also useful when the Palace decided to limit the numbers attending the mini-concert for Her Majesty. We then allowed entry by coloured ticket and avoided any embarrassment of having to turn away visitors who were simply having a look around and who stumbled on the entrance to the hall.

Never leave anything to chance, however small. If there is to be a plaque unveiling, someone should try out the mechanism before the curtains are pulled aside. It is amazing how often the drapes are put on at the last minute and then do not open properly. Having everything completed in a total dry run 24 hours before the actual ceremony was a major relief to us and we made some modifications as a result.

There is also the issue of the Royal pen! We now have a visitors' book that is signed by only two people; we bought it especially for the event. We deliberately did not buy a special writing implement. Having been warned of the problem, I filled my own fountain pen the day before the event and tried it out on the day. It was then handed over to the Royal couple. That way I was sure it would work; many people buy something new and discover that it malfunctions. Prince Philip said as much, stating that the pens offered never work and taking out his own. Her Majesty used mine. To my great relief, it all worked perfectly.

Ultimately, the visit itself went exactly to plan and I breathed a huge sigh of relief when the Royal couple departed. We then threw the gates open to allow anyone from Macclesfield to come into the grounds and enjoy the day. We even put on further performances of the music and dramatic performances. The grandmother of one of our pupils did not have a ticket, as they were limited to two per household. She was delighted to be able to be there after the event with her family. She waited outside the school grounds and saw the Queen depart – so she was happy.

It is very easy to take one's eye off the ball at times when one is working under so much pressure. I had got so bogged down in the details that it was only a week before the event that I realised how important this open access time would be *after* the Royal couple had left. We effectively had another Open Day on our hands, and needed to prepare accordingly. In the end, we had a supply of literature available in the hall and gave out dozens of prospectuses and lots of promotional material. Our registrations for admission showed a massive increase for the following year and we felt it was all worth the effort.

One of the words I got used to using throughout our memorable experience was: "Yes". Everyone was keen to be involved and we received all sorts of offers. For reasons I cannot remember, a company gave us dozens of balloons and blew them up for us. We gave them out to the children at the end of the day, which made everyone happy and produced a real party atmosphere.

Even the unexpected proved to be a bonus. Lots of people brought flowers for the Queen. Her Lady-in-Waiting was totally inundated and passed them on to the security men. We discovered the bouquets in our lodge at the end of the visit and wondered what to do with them. We could hardly give them back to donors, who had all left. Our caretaker then offered to take them to the local hospice, where they were exceptionally well received, as being more special than a normal bunch of flowers.

There were the inevitable issues about security. One expects it to be tight at these events, but in truth we were not ready for the number of security agencies with whom we had to liaise. We dealt with the local police, traffic organisations who were blocking the road and, of course, the Royals' personal security experts. These are the people who are normally on the edge of photographs and whom one sees on television.

However, we also dealt in addition with the security agents covering the premises, and others looking at logistics. In the end, one group stayed in the school overnight before the event and 'locked down' the whole school. Every door you approached had a NO ENTRY sign on it, with incredibly tough tape across it keeping it shut; the tape was really difficult to remove and lots of repainting occurred afterwards.

These people needed feeding too, of course, so our dining room suddenly sprang into action again – despite it being late July. The actual security on the day was very relaxed – presumably because all these people had done their job well. I will not forget asking one security man if he really needed to stop his van at a bottleneck position on our front drive a few days before the event. He assured me that he would only be two minutes, because he was taking an electronic signature of the school to compare with another to be taken just as the visit was about to start. I suddenly realised how sophisticated security has become these days.

Not every school will experience such a special event as we did – but the organisational principles which I have outlined can be applied to any opening of a major building, celebrity or VIP visit or other out-of-the-ordinary occasion. As with any major event in a school's life, the planning had to be an all-round team effort.

Through such experiences one gets to know one's senior managers much better than before – whether the Head decides to take the leading organisational role and (in order to create time for it) to delegate other day-to-day business to the deputies, or whether one of the SMT is given the specific task of organising the special event itself. All school leadership needs to be collaborative nowadays – but none more so than at a time when special demands are being made on the institution. It is also, of course, good experience to be carried forward into a future job by any deputy who later becomes a Head.

Would I do it all again? The visit occupied my life for over a year before the event and, mercifully, I went away for a good break two days after it. The only advice I would give to people in the same situation is this: make sure that a relaxing holiday is booked once the date is fixed. Of course, I would do it all again! I told the SMT that another visit in 500 years' time was certainly something I would relish! And there has been an additional bonus. The Lieutenancy rings us regularly and asks to use our fields to park the Royal helicopter. As such, I have been involved in three further Royal visits in the space of three years and I have become practised at dealing with 30-second conversations with a Royal as I guide them to the car. Now that sort of event I can happily live with!

Afterword

Brenda Despontin

The changing nature of school leadership has been covered extensively in recent educational literature, and was reflected in the essays on Headship in volume one of this series. Distributing leadership within a team, drawing on, and developing, the skills and competencies of each member, facilitates a more dynamic, effective and successful senior structure. The days of the autocratic despot are a distant memory, and the Head is now much more of a first among equals, with deputies given significant whole-school powers and responsibilities.

In this volume, the diversity of tasks within the deputy's remit is evident, defeating any chance of offering one definition or one single, transferable job description. One size cannot fit all schools: deputy/director of studies/senior teacher/second master/assistant head – even the nomenclature differs. As Gerald Ellison illustrates in his reflections on senior management teams, much will depend on the strengths and interests of the individuals. If it works, then let it!

Heads need senior teams they can trust: colleagues who are unafraid to challenge them in private whilst upholding a loyal party line in the staff room. Deputies can thus often walk a fine line between confidante to Head and conduit for the staff. 'Filtering' concerns, having excellent antennae, but knowing when to keep their own counsel make many deputies excellent candidates for the diplomatic corps, and it surprises me they are not headhunted for peace missions more frequently. Their skills may range from all the backroom detail for a Royal visit, as outlined in Stephen Coyne's chapter, or assisting with a disciplinary process as Nigel Richardson explains, or coping with the communal grief when a pupil dies, as I describe in my own chapter.

A wise Head and governing body will be sure that the deputies have input into any school development or business plan: after all, they will be on the front line in its delivery. Furthermore, both as a means of a better understanding of the 'bigger picture' *and* as part of their own continuous professional development, they should be given opportunities to learn about governance, and the financial and marketing strategies of their school. Christopher Jeffery talks of this competency, and an awareness of financial implications certainly helps when curriculum planning and management are part of a deputy's remit, illustrated in Paul Chapman's chapter.

For the curriculum deputy, an ability to manage heads of department will be crucial. Chapman cites the necessity to 'depersonalise', to engender debate, to chair effective meetings, to stimulate papers and academic discussion, to be familiar with inspection requirements and to prepare the school for its own. Heads of department are paid to fight their own corner, and earning their respect will require a deputy to acquire sound, relevant and recent knowledge of curriculum developments nationally, and the implications for the school of any proposals for change. In recent years the importance of data management has increased significantly, with greater emphasis on how it impacts on learning, so a high skills base in ICT and statistical analysis will be required too.

Those deputies or senior staff whose role has a focus on pastoral responsibilities face equally challenging duties, whether it be providing guidance for staff via the handbook, overseeing their induction and appraisal, or helping with appointments and interviews as Richard Backhouse reveals. A senior pastoral manager who is head of boarding will experience any number of difficult and demanding scenarios, as Carol Richards highlights, and pastoral deputies often oversee policies, procedures, child welfare, school council and disciplinary issues as detailed by Charlotte Avery.

Sometimes, greatness is thrust unexpectedly upon a deputy and Thomas Packer's honest account provides a useful insight into how such crises evolve, and what the outcome can be. Daphne West talks wisely of protected time as essential for deputies to work effectively. Sometimes they can feel themselves to be under siege from all quarters, and are too visible and available – much more so than the Head, protected fiercely as (s)he is by a well-trained Rottweiler PA.

The profession of deputy headship deserves a regular training programme – and dedicated school funding for it. The HMC/GSA/SHMIS courses from IPD are varied, topical and relevant, but each deputy's individual training needs should be identified and agreed formally, via a structured, regular appraisal, preferably 360° with input from those line-managed. It may be that the deputy has no ambition to progress to Headship, but wishes to acquire skills to timetable or to analyse MIDYIS data to assist teaching and learning in the school. Others will be seeking the necessary fillip to Headship, and should be encouraged, possibly part-financed, to obtain an MBA in Educational Leadership, or the NPQH.

If deputies have spent years in the same school and been promoted internally, it will be of huge benefit to visit other schools or even to shadow a Head elsewhere, to nurture some 'out of the box' thinking. David Pacini mentions these experiences in his chapter – but is at pains to remind those aspiring to a senior post that they should *enjoy* the opportunity to make a difference in a school. Mercifully, it is not limited to dealing solely with the complaints which Helen Wright details, so familiar to us all. She describes the difficult 'people stuff' which keeps us awake at night because there are no quick fixes at our disposal: tricky demons like staff incompetence, or suspicions of child protection issues. She reminds us of the importance of remaining calm with fractious, unreasonable parents, and she shares with us the words of Dale Carnegie which I have since pinned to my desk: 'Any fool can criticise, condemn and complain, but it takes character and self control to be understanding and forgiving.'

Those who support the Head in any one of a range of senior roles need in abundance those qualities which Carnegie quotes: the *character* to adjust chameleon-like to the different demands of staffroom and boardroom; the *self-control* to feign ignorance when pressed for gossip, or the patience when the Head proposes yet another impractical new initiative. A deputy will be *understanding* of a Head's pressures and foibles and, yes, *forgiving* of the occasions when the hours of meticulous planning and the sleepless nights ahead of a Royal visit or an inspection seem to go unnoticed.

I am sure I have never thanked my deputies anywhere near enough. Without their wisdom, honesty, loyalty, kindness, laughter and love I would never have stayed in post as long, and I owe so much to their tireless efforts. It has been a privilege to share the leadership journey with such inspiring professionals, and I hope the chapters in this volume will encourage others to join a leadership team, and experience first hand the satisfaction it holds.